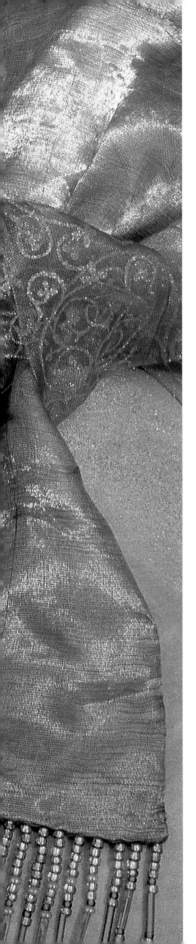

beading

projects · techniques · motifs

Diana Vernon

Photography by Linda Burgess

Quadrille

page 2: Fringed Bag (see page 57)
page 3: Beaded Cuff links (see page 42)

Detail photography · Peter Cassidy, Dave King
Illustrations · Tim Pearce
Technical drawings · Stephen Dew

This edition first published in 2005 by
Quadrille Publishing Limited
Alhambra House
27–31 Charing Cross Road
London WC2H 0LS

Originally published in association with Country Living, a trademark of the National Magazine Company Limited.

Publishing Director Anne Furniss
Art Director Mary Evans
Managing Editor Jane O'Shea
Editor Carey Smith
Copy Editor Sarah Widdicombe
Art Editor Alison Shakleton
Production Assistant Kate Walford

British Library Cataloguing-in-Publication Data
A catalogue record for this book is available from the British Library

ISBN 1 84400 271 3

Printed in China

beading

contents

Introduction

The allure of beads in all their myriad shapes, sizes and colours has captivated our aesthetic and tactile senses since prehistoric peoples first threaded bones and shells onto thongs and animal sinews to adorn their bodies.

For many centuries, beads have been used as a focus for prayer and contemplation, as with the mala string of prayer beads used by Hindus and Buddhists and the rosary used by Christian worshippers. Many other religions also use some form of prayer beads – the word 'bead' itself is thought to be derived from the Old English gebed or bedu and the Middle English bede, all of which mean prayer. Even without a spiritual focus, many a nervous person seeking calm has fiddled with their pearls or string of 'worry beads'!

The earliest beads were made from clay, stone, shells (such as the wampum made and used by North American Indians) and semi-precious stones. The Egyptians developed a special clay recipe called 'faience', or Egyptian paste, and the beads created by this process were worked into the collars worn by the Pharoahs. Beads are depicted in wall paintings and discovered in the pyramids.

It is believed that one of the first applications of glassmaking was in the manufacture of glass beads. These were produced in such quantities that they became an important item for trade and developed into a worldwide currency. These beads became known as 'trade-wind' or 'pony' beads, and the beading of North American Indians and African nations preserved from this time demonstrates the artistry and skill with which they were worked.

Before this, medieval embroiderers in Europe had been incorporating drilled pearls, coral and semi-precious gemstones into their work. Later, during the Tudor and Stuart periods, glass beads and pearls were used in great abundance to decorate embroidery and to embellish costume. Then in the mid-nineteenth century the Victorians developed a real passion for decorating items of interior furnishing with beading. This enthusiasm was no doubt fuelled by the repeal of the Glass Tax in 1845 which made glass affordable again.

This book aims to demonstrate the glory of beads and to continue a rich tradition which has been preserved from time immemorial.

Starting to bead

Beading is an age-old technique and an exciting, visual and tactile craft. This book deals mainly with beading using a needle and thread, perhaps the easiest form of beading of all. With no major equipment to worry about, it is a craft which is easily portable: if you are pressed for time, your design can be picked up, carried with you and worked when time allows.

Some of the ideas in this book are so easy that a young child could have a go; others are slightly more complex and involve careful charting. Once you have mastered the basic techniques, such as a beaded triangle for a bookmark or a picot drop for a cushion edging, you might well feel inspired to create something more ambitious – a beaded curtain or wall-hanging perhaps. This chapter presents some simple but effective ideas for needlewoven beading.

the beads

Naming and describing beads can often be problematic, as the same bead may be given different names in different places. Even individual bead merchants may call similar stock by a variety of names. Often, beads have been given a name which is derived from a very old trade name and sometimes, especially if this name has been abbreviated, the original may be lost. For example, the beautiful iridescent, metallic beads now called '3 cut' – because of their 3-cut, faceted exterior – used to be known as 'lofo' or 'Kashmir' but nobody knows why. Even now, when those selling the beads retire, if there are no records the origins of the names are quite often lost.

Rocailles

Two commonly used small beads are 'rocailles' and 'seed beads'. Technically, a rocaille is oblate – that is, a sphere flattened at its poles – while a seed bead is completely round. ('Rocaille' is a French word meaning 'little rock', and an architectural Style Rocaille, which later became Rococo – based on rounded lines, such as rocks and shells – was in fashion during the reign of Louis XV.)

Many bead merchants now describe all small glass beads, including seed beads, as rocailles, since most are not completely spherical or round. However, aware of the confusion, some merchants' catalogues now list only 'small glass beads' rather than referring to rocailles or seed beads, so these terms might disappear in due course.

Old trade names you may come across include Tosca, faceted on the outside, with a square hole; Charlotte, faceted on the outside, with a round hole; Pompadour, larger, with a large hole (traditional for lace bobbins); Pound, rocailles once sold by weight; 3 cut, with 3 cuts or facets on the outside; and 2 cut (2 cuts or facets on the outside).

Opaque
These are of one solid colour, and may have a polished, matt or chalky finish.

Transparent
There are four different varieties of transparent rocailles:
Plain transparent.
Colour-lined transparent, where a pale colour or clear bead is lined with a second colour, thus producing an attractive bicoloured effect.

Silver-lined transparent, where the bead is lined with silver and usually has a square-cut hole to reflect the silver with greater intensity.

Transparent with iridescent finish, usually called 'iris' and sometimes 'rainbow' or 'ab', the latter an abbreviation of 'aurora borealis'.

Pearlized
These have a pearly finish to the glass, not a pearl 'skin' (see Pearls, below).

Lustre
These rocailles have a high, often metallic, gloss finish.

Metallic As the name suggests, these rocailles have a metallic finish.

Bugles

Bugles are glass tubes mainly available in sizes 2mm to 30mm. There are three profiles: round with a round hole, round with a square hole, and faceted with a round hole. The finishes available are similar to those for rocailles.

Pearls

Artificial
Artificial pearls are available in round, oat, drop and fancy shapes (usually flower and leaf). They come in white, ivory and pastel shades, as well as gold and silver. The pearl finish is a 'skin' of varnish and the beads should be handled carefully.

Mother-of-pearl
This variety of pearl is formed from oyster shells.

Natural
Natural pearls are available in round and 'baroque' (irregular) shapes. They are, however, very expensive, so allow for this in your design costing.

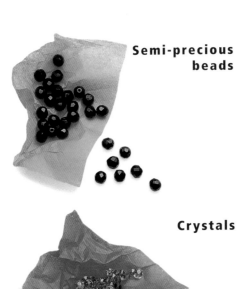

Semi-precious beads

Some semi-precious stones are easier to drill than others: garnet, quartz, amber, jet, moonstone, coral and jade are some of those most often used.

NB Jet, the fossillized mineral, is very soft and brittle and is therefore not an ideal material for beads as it can shatter. If you see 'jet' beads described in a catalogue, they are most likely to be made from black glass and manganese.

(This combination is often called 'French jet', possibly from the word *jais*, the French for jet, which is the term embroiderers' once used to describe beads in general – in a seventeenth-century book by the embroiderer Charles Saint Aubin, he describes bead embroidery as *La Broderie en Jais*.) However, if the 'jet' is warm to the touch, the beads may well be real jet.

Crystals

Natural crystal quartz beads are available, but the term usually refers to cut-glass beads and drops. These come in a variety of shapes and cuts of facet, and in many beautiful colours. Often, some of the facets will be mirror finished to increase the sparkle effect,

while the shapes available include 'marguerites' (daisy shapes) and hearts.

Other crystals which can be incorporated with beading are 'loc rosen', which are embroidery stones with a flat back, faceted surface and central hole.

Metal beads

It is possible to buy gold and silver beads, which are often plated. Brass, copper and other metal beads are also

available and can be very effective, but it is wise to consider whether they will tarnish or be too heavy for the thread.

Specials and found beads

There are many beautiful beads available, including hand-blown glass beads, Venetian glass and lampwork beads (where trails of molten glass are trickled around a bead or flower, or dot designs are formed). There are also Chinese lacquer, Japanese magatama, which are rocailles with an off-centre hole, and beads made from perfumed wax – a good book on pot-pourri will explain how. It is worth hunting for

specials at antique fairs and in bric-à-brac shops. Look through old jewellery and button boxes, too: many a broken necklace has been relegated to the button box and you may find a real treasure. You will also find beads made from clay, wood, paper and plastics, as well as from natural objects such as seeds, nuts, bamboo and shells. You can drill your own found objects using a fine modelmaker's drill with care.

Dyeing beads

It is possible to dye some small glass beads and pearls. Bead merchants will dye beads for you if you need a large quantity, but for small amounts it is easy to do yourself. Experiment to see how the dye takes on the different types.

You will need
French enamel varnish (FEV)
Methylated spirit
Small bowl or jam jar
Beads
Pencil or chopstick
White tissue paper

1 Mix one part FEV with two parts methylated spirit in a jar or bowl. These proportions are approximate; for some beads, you may need more varnish.

2 If the beads are not pre-strung, string them on to a thread, submerge them in the mixture and swish around.
3 Using the end of a pencil or chopstick, lift the beads carefully out of the dye. Lay them on a piece of tissue paper and gently pat off the excess dye, then hang up to dry naturally.
NB If dyeing pearls, lift them from the dye, and then hang up immediately to dry. Do not pat dry, as the pearl varnish 'skin' may become damaged.

other equipment

Most beading techniques involve very little in the way of tools and materials, but here are some basic guidelines to help you get started. Beading need not be an expensive craft – many of these materials you might find you already have at home.

The current interest in beads and beading is reflected in the expanding number of specialist bead shops and mail-order bead companies. Unusual and interesting beads have never been more widely available.

Working board

You will need a board on which to pin out flat needlewoven beading and fringing while it is being worked. A piece of cork board, or the fibre board often known as macramé board, is ideal, although a thick cork tile or piece of polystyrene will work just as well so long as it provides a firm surface.

If leaving work pinned to a board for any length of time, it is advisable to cover with a piece of cloth or tissue paper to keep it dust free.

Needles

Beading needles are available in several sizes, but being very long and fine they tend to bend and break easily. You may find the finer sizes of 'straw' needles (for example sizes 8 and 9), often used in millinery work, more reliable.

It is possible to make your own needles by bending a piece of fine wire, such as fuse wire, and twisting the ends together to form an 'eye' of whatever size you require, but this only works well with larger beads. Using the wire bent double and not twisted, but held tightly together in the fingers, is sometimes a successful ploy.

There are no hard-and-fast rules for selecting appropriate needles, so it is best to experiment. Try the particular bead hole on the needle, remembering to allow for the thickness of the thread used and the fact that a bead will usually have a needle passed through it twice during needleweaving – this means that the hole must be able to accommodate four thicknesses of the thread used.

Threads

There are many fine yet strong threads now available, but polyester thread is one, for example, which is particularly useful for beading.

Test the strength of a thread by trying to break it by pulling tightly. Synthetic fishing line and some nylon threads are strong, but are hard to control while working as they are quite springy. Waxed linen carpet thread and buttonhole thread are good for threading beads for fringing if they have large enough holes.

Running a thread over a block of beeswax will increase its tensile strength, and is useful when threading bugles and some faceted beads, as they tend to have very sharp edges. With beads with smaller holes, there can be disadvantages in that the wax is scraped off the thread as it passes through the bead hole and gathers between the beads, smearing the finished beadwork. Again, it is best to experiment to discover the methods that work well in each instance.

Wire

For the wire beading projects in this book (see Pin and wire beading chapter), you can use electrical (tinned copper) fuse wire. Wires with diameters of 0.345mm and 0.213mm are useful for small beads. Gold, silver and some beautiful rainbow colours are to be found in fishing fly-tying wire.

Containers

It is helpful to store your beads in clear glass jars. For small quantities, little individual jam pots are good, while fishing-tackle boxes and the small partitioned boxes used for screws, nails and so on are ideal for storing crystals and other specials.

Transfer the beads you are using to shallow dishes or saucers. The little china dishes used for mixing watercolour paint, or the plastic palettes sectioned into different-sized areas which are used for Chinese brush painting, are both excellent for this. Whatever you use, be sure that there is enough space in the dish to allow you to pick up the bead you need on to the needle easily.

A piece of corrugated cardboard is useful for laying down a row of beads to see if you are happy with the overall effect; there are also bead-stringing boards available designed specifically for this purpose.

Other useful tools

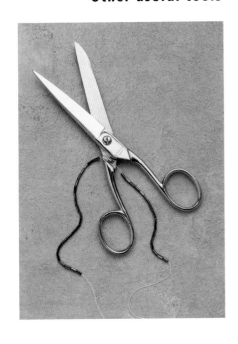

All-metal scissors
These are useful for breaking off a particular bead – perhaps because it is cracked or chipped – from a strung thread without needing to unthread all the beads.

Tweezers
Tweezers are helpful in selecting a particular bead from a mixed pack.

Double-sided sticky tape
This can be stuck on to your working surface and used to secure beads, needles and pins ready for use.

Thimble
Special thimbles are available with a tacky, bobbly surface (similar to banknote-counting thimbles) which enables you to pick up beads without dropping them.

Glass-headed pins
Coloured glass-headed pins can be used to mark particular sequences of threading and to count the number of beads in a row or round. To use in this way, slip the pin through the hole in the threaded bead.

Jeweller's pliers
Cut small pieces of felt and glue them to the jaws of these small pliers, so that if you need to coax a needle through a bead you can do so without scoring the surface of the needle. Use very carefully, as too much pressure could result in a cracked bead.

Handy hints

• If the beads you have bought are pre-strung, as they are for tambour bead embroidery (a method of attaching beads to fabric with a small hook), it is helpful to keep them on the string and transfer them on to the needle straight from it, especially if you are using a number of the same beads.

• If you need a number of the same colour bead from loose beads – for instance, if you are working a length of fringe – instead of trying to locate each bead hole individually with the needle, use the following method. Pour the beads into a deep dish (a wooden salad bowl is ideal), thread a needle and, bouncing the bowl gently on your knees, plunge the needle rhythmically in and out of the bowl: the beads will jump on to the needle without your having to peer tediously at each individual hole. This is the traditional method used in Venice by the bead threaders, who used the technique while holding 20 or more needles fanned out in their hands. Try it – it does work!

needlewoven beading

This is a method of interlacing beads with a needle and one length of thread. It is an extremely versatile technique, which can be used for creating flat, one-dimensional objects, or shaped, three-dimensional items. Because this technique forms a structure of beads placed between beads, rather than on top of each other as in loomwoven beading, it is sometimes described as diagonal beadweaving due to the way the positioning of the beads lends itself to diagonal patterns. You can use this to advantage in your choice of colour schemes. For information on how to chart a design see pages 98–99.

Starting off

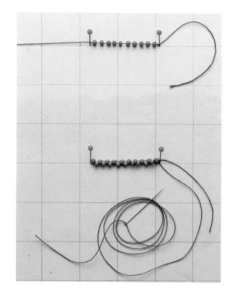

This is the basic technique, but by varying the numbers of beads in rows, and changing the threading sequence, it is possible to create different effects which you will be shown how to work in later chapters.

1 Make a 'base' row of beads, either by stitching the beads on to a piece of fabric, or by stringing them out on to a corkboard between two securing pins – one at each end – to hold the 'base' or 1st row.

2 Pass needle and thread through 1st bead of 1st row, then thread a loose single bead and pass needle and thread through next bead of 1st row, adjacent to the one you have just gone through.

3 In effect you are hanging each bead of 2nd row between pairs of beads of 1st row. The edge bead hangs in alternate rows (see the coloured bead in fig 1).

4 The 3rd row of beads will hang between pairs of beads of 2nd row, and so on (fig 2), continuing the sequence as in 1st 2 rows.

fig 1

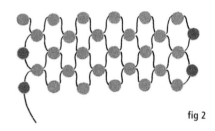

fig 2

Openwork beading

By threading more than one bead on to your needle, and passing the needle and thread through, for instance, every other pair of beads of the previous row, you can create openwork, lace and honeycomb effects. By combining this method with simple beaded drops, you can work a variety of interesting decorative trims.

Also, by careful shaping of the structure, by increasing and decreasing the number and/or size of the beads used, a three-dimensional effect can be achieved.

Beaded triangle finish

If you decrease each row by one bead, you will create a triangular shape which, when finished off with a drop, makes an interesting trim, or edging when repeated. This is the method used to embellish the cushion on page 21. It is equally effective when used singly, as opposite in the beaded bookmark.

Bead picot finish

The simplest way to attach a drop or to finish a string of bead fringing is to use a single bead (fig 3), by threading on a larger drop after the last bead of work, or, for a fringed item, threading on a small bead (the 'anchor' bead), and passing the needle up through the drop or the last bead of the fringing.

The bead picot finish is used to give an added richness to the beaded drop (fig 4) by threading on 4 beads and passing the needle through the first bead threaded of the 4. When the thread is pulled up firmly the 3 beads will form a 'picot'.

fig 3   fig 4

Beaded bookmark

You will need

35cm (14in) moiré ribbon, 5cm (2in) wide
1m (1¼yd) polyester thread
Needle fine enough to pass through beads twice when threaded
39 iridescent blue beads (iri bl bd)
21 large gold rocailles (lg gld roc)
1 drop bead

To make

1 Lightly draw a line in soft pencil on to back of ribbon, about 5cm (2in) from end, and stitch 10 iri bl bd to ribbon width from right to left on right side, using reverse side line as a guide.

2 Turn up ribbon and then pin wrong sides together.

3 Continue to work beading following chart (fig 1), i.e. 2nd row, working left to right, pass needle back through 1st bead stitched (A) to ribbon on 1st row and begin to interlace beads to this base row as follows: 2 iri bl bd, 1 lg gld roc, 3 iri bl bd, 1 lg gld roc, 2 iri bl bd; then pass needle back through 1st bead (B) threaded to begin to work 3rd row.

4 When you have worked to single iri bl bd at row 10, thread 1 lg gld roc, 1 drop bead, 1 iri bl bd, 3 lge gld roc; pass needle up through the iri bl bd, drop bead and lg gld roc and work a fastening-off stitch to secure (see below). Thread back down through beads and cut off neatly.

5 Turn in ribbon to form a hem and handstitch down, neatly repeating this turned and stitched hem at top of bookmark.

6 Cover carefully with layers of tissue paper or a pressing cloth and press with a cool iron, avoiding beading at the bottom edge.

This shows the principle of the fastening-off stitch. Pass needle under thread forming a loop below the bead thread. Take needle over top of bead thread into loop. Pull very tightly.

The same stitch is used as a concealed fastening-on stitch by making a small stitch under fabric to create a loop, or passing needle and thread through some beads to conceal tail of thread.

The fastening-off stitch shown here applied to a string of beads.

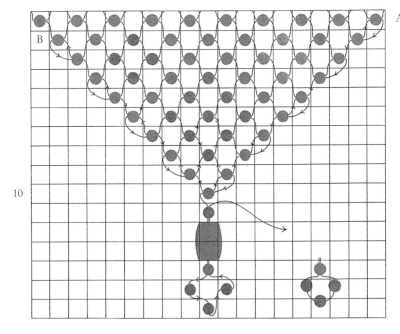

fig 1

beaded trims

Beaded trims can give a rich, decorative effect to a variety of interior and fashion-related projects. Designing simple trims gives an opportunity to study the different effects that can be created by varying the colour palette, the number and sizes of beads and the threading sequence. Experimenting with different combinations of these elements will enable you to design more elaborate and visually interesting beadwork.

   All three cushions in this next project are trimmed on two opposite edges, so the bead quantities given here reflect this.

Wine silk cushion

You will need
40cm (16in) square cushion
Polyester thread
Needle fine enough to pass through
   beads twice when threaded
280 iridescent amber rocailles
   (iri amb roc)
140 8mm pink bugles (8m pk bg)
132 crimson rocailles (crm roc)
84 orange rocailles (org roc)
82 large gold rocailles (lg gld roc)
54 large crimson rocailles (lg crm roc)
42 purple barrel-shaped beads
   (pur b-s bd)
40 4mm-diam garnet beads
   (4m gnt bd)

22 8mm amethyst bugles
   (8m ame bg)
22 6mm-diameter yellow crystals
   (6m yell crs)
20 6mm-diam amethyst crystals
   (6m ame crs)
20 6mm brown bugles
   (6m br bg)
12 8mm-diam dark amethyst faceted
   crystals (8m dk ame fc crs)
11 5mm-diam amber beads
   (5m amb bd)
10 8mm-diam dark amber faceted
   crystals (8m dk amb fc crs)
10 5mm-diam garnet beads (5m gnt bd)

To make up
1 Using pins as markers, measure one edge and at centre point push in a pin vertically to mark it. Working from this centre point, to both left and right of it mark each 2cm (¾in) point. You will then have a total of 21 pins to be used as markers.
2 Starting at either left or right side seamline, begin to work edging. Note that the following instructions assume that you are working from left to right.
3 Working long drop Thread 1 lg crm roc, 1 5m amb bd, 1 lg gld roc, 1 pur b-s bd, 1 org roc, 1 8m ame bg, 1 crm roc, 1 6m yel crs, 1 lg crm roc, 1 8m dk ame fc crs, 1 org roc; then pass needle up through all beads threaded before last org roc. This will then form the long drop. Pull thread to ensure that drop hangs straight and make a small fastening-off stitch to secure. Thread your needle invisibly through seam stitching and then advance one bead width to the right.

4 Working in-between beading Thread 1 iri amb roc, 1 crm roc, 1 8m pk bg, 1 lg gld roc, 1 4m gnt bd, 3 iri amb roc; then pass needle up through 1 4m gnt bd and lg gld roc. This will form a picot of the 3 iri amb roc. Now stitch into seamline one bead width to left of next pin marker, and make a small fastening-off stitch to secure. Now thread needle invisibly through seam line, emerging again at next pin marker.
5 Working shorter drop Thread 1 lg gld roc, 1 pur b-s bd, 1 org roc, 1 6m br bg, 1 lg crm roc, 1 8m pk bg, 1 org roc, 1 6m ame crs, 1 crm roc; then pass needle up through 1st 8 beads and bugle threaded. This will form the shorter drop and there will be 10 of these in total. Pull thread so that drop hangs straight and make a small fastening-off stitch to secure. Again advance invisibly through seamline, one bead width to the right, to repeat previous bead threading sequence, which is repeated between each drop (fig 1).

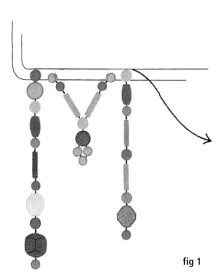
fig 1

6 Working second long drop Thread 1 org roc, 1 5m gnt bd, 1 lg gld roc, 1 pur b-s bd, 1 org roc, 1 8m ame bg, 1 crm roc, 1 8m dk amb fc crs, 1 crm roc; then pass needle up through all beads before last crm roc and continue as for 1st long drop.

7 Continue working with in-between beading, short drop (all identical), in-between beading, 1st long drop and so on. The cushion edge beading will be as illustrated (fig 2).

fig 2

8 The finishing step To give a continuous beaded effect along seamline of cushion, between each 'between the drops' beading sequence, thread 1 iri amb roc, 1 8m pk bg, 1 iri amb roc, and stitch down, threading invisibly along seamline to next point 'between the drops' (fig 3).

9 Repeat all instructions given above to work beaded edging on opposite side of cushion.

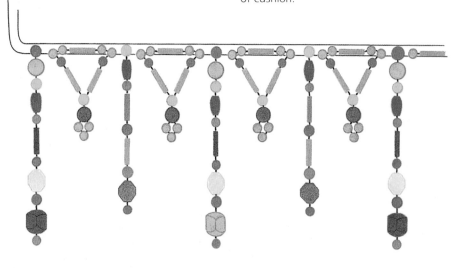

fig 3

Gold silk cushion

You will need

40cm (16in) square cushion
80cm (32in) bronze or gold metallic
  ribbon, 5cm (2in) wide
Gold metallic thread, polyester thread
Needle fine enough to pass through
  beads twice when threaded
240 iridescent gold rocailles (iri gld roc)
40 iridescent amber rocailles (iri amb roc)
36 orange rocailles (org roc)

26 5mm-diam bronze faceted beads
  (5m brz fc bd)
22 large gold rocailles (lg gld roc)
14 5mm-diam amber beads (5m amb bd)
10 1cm-diam yellow crystals (1cm yel crs)
8 8mm-diam amber faceted beads
  (8m amb fc bd)
6 bronze rocailles (brz roc)
4 6mm-diam amber faceted beads
  (6m amb fc bd)

To make up

Before the beading is worked a gathered ribbon trim is stitched to the two edges.

1 Prepare ribbon by rolling and oversewing each raw end with gold metallic sewing thread, then run a gathering stitch down one selvedge edge of ribbon. Pin middle of ribbon to middle point of cushion edge. Pin one end to left edge and the other to right edge.

2 Pull up gathering thread, stroking ribbon into neat gathers as you go. Then pin ribbon down to cushion edge every few centimetres (inches), stitch securely using small stitches and fasten off neatly. You are now ready to work the beaded trim.

3 Using pins as markers (fig 2), measure one edge and at centre point E, push in a pin vertically to mark it. Mark left point A and right point I side seams in the same way.

4 At points A, E and I work a long drop. Thread 1 brz roc, 1 5m amb bd, 1 1cm yel crs, 1 6m amb fc bd, 1 lg gld roc, 10 iri gld roc, 1 org roc, 1 5m brz fc bd, 3 org roc; pass needle up after last 3 org roc; 1 5m brz fc bd, 1 org roc; then thread 10 iri gld roc and pass needle up through 1st beads threaded, pull thread neatly so that drop hangs straight (fig 1), and make a fastening-off stitch.

5 Measure middle point between centre and both sides, and mark again with a pin. Mark also 1.5cm (⅝in) to the right of left side mark, 1.5cm (⅝in) to the left of right side mark and 1.5cm (⅝in) on either side of centre point (fig 2).

6 At points B and H work a drop. Thread 1 org roc, 1 5m brz fc bd, 1 iri gld roc, 1 8m amb fc bd, 1 org roc, 1 1cm yel crs, 1 org roc, 1 8m amb fc bd, 1 iri gld roc; pass needle up through the 1 5m brz fc bd and 1 org roc, pull into a circular drop and fasten off (fig 3).

7 Measure centre point between C and D and F and G, and mark with pins.

8 Begin now at point C. Thread 1 lg gld roc, 7 iri gld roc, 1 iri amb roc, 1 5m amb bd, 3 iri amb roc; pass needle up through the 1 5m amb bd and 1 iri amb roc. Thread 7 iri gld roc, 1 lg gld roc and stitch into middle point between C and D. Thread 1 iri amb roc, 1 5m brz fc bd, 1 iri amb roc; pass needle up through 1st 2 beads threaded and stitch again through middle point; repeat previous threading and stitch to point D (fig 4).

9 Repeat another set of beading as shown in fig 4 between points F and G.

10 Repeat instructions to work opposite side of cushion.

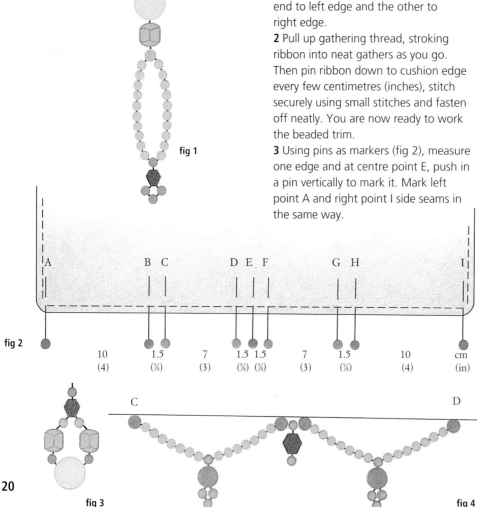

fig 1

fig 2

| A | | 10 (4) | | B | C | 1.5 (⅝) | | 7 (3) | | D | E | F | 1.5 (⅝) | 1.5 (⅝) | | 7 (3) | | G | H | 1.5 (⅝) | | 10 (4) | | I | cm (in) |

fig 3

fig 4

Yellow brocade cushion

You will need

28cm (11in) square cushion
Polyester thread
Needle fine enough to pass through
   beads twice when threaded
248 large iridescent turquoise rocailles
   (lg iri turq roc)

126 large gold rocailles (lg gld roc)
104 orange rocailles (org roc)
10 8mm-diam turquoise faceted crystals
   (8m turq fc crs)
8 5mm-diam turquoise crystals
   5m turq crs)

To make up

This cushion is trimmed with the beaded triangle as seen on page 15, this time repeated as an edging.

1 Using pins as markers, measure and mark one edge as shown in fig 1.

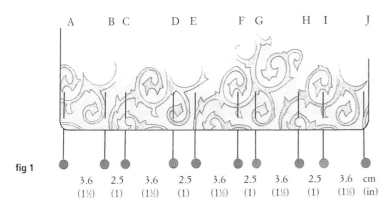

A   B C   D E   F G   H I   J

| 3.6 | 2.5 | 3.6 | 2.5 | 3.6 | 2.5 | 3.6 | 2.5 | 3.6 | cm |
| (1½) | (1) | (1½) | (1) | (1½) | (1) | (1½) | (1) | (1½) | (in) |

fig 1

2 Starting at either left or right side seamline, begin to work the edging. The following instructions assume you are working from left to right.

3 To work 1st triangle, stitch 7 lg iri turq roc evenly to cushion edge between points A and B, then pass needle back through last bead stitched to work 2nd row. Thread 1 lg iri turq roc, 1 lg gld roc,

1 iri turq roc, 1 iri turq roc, 1 lg gld roc, 1 lg iri turq roc between each pair of lg iri turq roc of 1st row. Following fig 2, continue to work rest of triangle, finishing with 8m turq fc crs and bead picot as shown. Work one of these triangles between points C and D, E and F, G and H, I and J.

4 Now restart thread at point B, and measure and mark with pins 7 equal spaces to point C: each space will accommodate one bead.

5 Working from point B to point C, thread 3 org roc and stitch into seam at 2nd pin, in order to form an org roc picot. Now stitch 1 lg iri turq roc, 1 lg gld roc, 1 lg iri turq roc between next 3 pins and then pass needle back through last bead stitched.

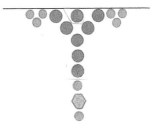

fig 3

6 Interlace 1 lg iri turq roc, then another, and continue to work beading following fig 3. When the 5m turq crs and 1 org bead have been threaded, pass needle up through the 5m turq crs and rest of beading to work next 3 org roc picot.

7 Run thread invisibly through seamline to point D and work the same sequence (steps 5 and 6) between points D and E, F and G, H and I.

8 Repeat all instructions given above to work beaded edging on opposite side of cushion.

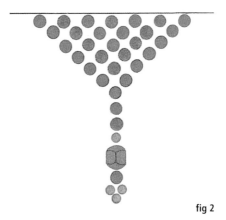

fig 2

21

grapes & vineleaves

The striking vineleaves incorporated into these two chokers are an unusual example of the openwork or beaded lace technique described on page 14. Used here to create an interesting three-dimensional effect, it is combined with two methods of bead threading to create the bunches of bead 'grapes'. The same methods can also be used to make clusters of beads forming decorative drops to be used as trims for cushions, tie-backs, or as edgings for garments and soft furnishings.

The basic pattern for the two chokers seen here is identical.

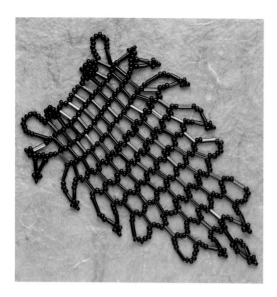

You will need

Polyester thread

Needle fine enough to pass through beads and bugles twice when threaded

For crystal choker:

40cm (16in) approx velvet ribbon (or take your neck measurement), 1.5cm (⅝in) wide; add 5cm (2in) for finishing

4cm (1½in) velcro fastening

Vineleaf beads:

  463 green rocailles (roc)

  101 6mm iridescent green bugles (bg)

  15 4mm iridescent green bugles (sm bg)

Grape beads:

  10 1cm-diam pink faceted crystals

  6 1cm-diam purple/petrol blue faceted beads

Grape stems:

  38 pink crystal rocailles

  36 purple rocailles

  18 4mm pink bugles

  16 6mm iridescent purple bugles

For garnet choker:

Ribbon and velcro fastening: as for crystal choker

Vineleaf beads: as for crystal choker

Grape beads:

  46 5mm-diam garnet or purple glass beads

Grape stems:

  23 small bronze metallic beads

  15 small amber glass beads

  4 6mm bronze bugles

  2 large amber beads

  1 pinky bronze bead

  1 green-bronze bead

To work vineleaves for both chokers

1 Prepare the thread. Cut a 3m (3¼yd) length and find centre point by placing ends together. Make an overhand knot and slip a pin into it before pulling thread tight. Push pin into your cork board to secure the thread.

2 You will work right-hand side of vineleaf first, so thread a needle on to one end of thread and carefully place end without needle to left-hand side of board, while you are working with needle-threaded length.

To work right-hand side

Work from centre to right-hand side edge as follows:

1st row (fig 1) Thread 1 bg, 1 roc, 1 bg, 1 roc, 1 bg, 1 roc, 1 bg, 2 roc, 1 bg, 2 roc, 1 bg, 2 roc, 1bg, 2 roc, 1 bg, 3 roc, 1 bg, 3 roc, 1 bg, 3 roc, 1 bg, 3 roc, 1 sm bg, 4 roc. Now make a picot of last 3 beads by passing needle up through 4th last bead of this row.

2nd row (fig 2) This row will begin to shape the 'lace' structure and it will become progressively easier to work. Thread 1 sm bg, 3 roc; pass needle up through bugle K of 1st row; 3 roc, 1 bg, 3 roc; pass needle up through bugle I of 1st row; 3 roc, 1 bg, 2 roc; pass needle up through bugle G of 1st row, 2 roc, 1 bg, 2 roc; pass needle up through bugle E of 1st row; 2 roc, 1 bg, 1 roc; pass needle up through bugle C of 1st row; 1 roc, 1 bg, 1 roc; pass needle up through bugle A of 1st row.

3rd row (fig 3) Thread 2 roc, 1 bg, 1 roc; pass needle down through bugle B of 2nd row; 1 roc, 1 bg, 1 roc; pass needle down through bugle D of 2nd row; 2 roc, 1 bg, 2 roc; pass needle down through bugle F of 2nd row; 2 roc, 1 bg, 2 roc; pass needle down through bugle H of 2nd row; 3 roc, 1 bg, 3 roc; pass needle down through bugle J of 2nd row; 3 roc, 1 sm bg, 4 roc. Make a picot of last 3 beads by passing needle up through 4th last bead of this row.

4th row (fig 4) Thread 1 sm bg, 3 roc, 1 bg, 3 roc; pass needle up through bugle I of 3rd row; 3 roc, 1 bg, 2 roc; pass needle up through bugle G of 3rd row; 2 roc, 1 bg, 2 roc; pass needle up through bugle E of 3rd row; 2 roc, 1 bg, 1 roc; pass needle up through bugle C of 3rd row; 1 roc, 1 bg, 1 roc; pass needle up through bugle A of 3rd row.

5th row (fig 5) Thread 3 roc, 1 bg, 1 roc; pass needle down through bugle B of 4th row; 1 roc, 1 bg, 1 roc; pass needle down through bugle D of 4th row; 2

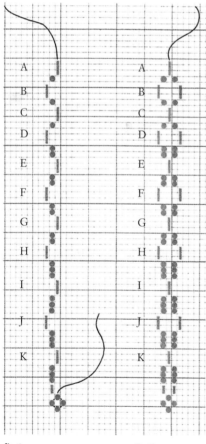

fig 1   fig 2

roc, 1 bg, 2 roc; pass needle down through bugle F of 4th row; 2 roc, 1 bg, 2 roc; pass needle down through bugle H of 4th row; 3 roc, 1 bg, 3 roc; pass needle down through bugle J of 4th row.

6th row (fig 6) Thread 5 roc, 1 bg, 3 roc; pass needle up through bugle I of 5th row; 3 roc, 1 bg, 2 roc; pass needle up through bugle G of 5th row; 2 roc, 1 bg, 2 roc; pass needle up through bugle E of 5th row; 2 roc, 1 bg, 1 roc; pass needle up through bugle C of 5th row; 1 roc, 1 bg, 1 roc; pass needle up through bugle A of 5th row.

7th row (fig 7) Thread 5 roc, 1 bg, 1 roc; pass needle down through bugle B of 6th row; 1 roc, 1 bg, 1 roc; pass needle down through bugle D of 6th row; 2 roc, 1 bg, 2 roc; pass needle down through bugle F of 6th row; 2 roc, 1 bg, 2 roc; pass needle down through bugle H of 6th row.

8th row (fig 8) Thread 7 roc, 1 bg, 2 roc; pass needle up through bugle G of 7th row; 2 roc, 1 bg, 2 roc; pass needle up through bugle E of 7th row; 2 roc, 1 bg, 1 roc; pass needle up through bugle C of 7th row; 1 roc, 1 bg, 1 roc; now pass needle up through bugle A of 7th row.

9th row Thread 8 roc, 1 bg, 1 roc; pass needle down through bugle B of 8th row; 1 roc, 1 bg, 1 roc; pass needle down through bugle D of 8th row; 2 roc, 1 bg, 2 roc; pass needle down through bugle F of 8th row; 3 roc, 1 sm bg, 4 roc. Now make a picot of last 3 beads by passing needle up through 4th last bead of this row.

10th row Thread 1 sm bg, 3 roc, 1 bg, 2 roc; pass needle up through bugle E of 9th row; 2 roc, 1 bg, 1 roc; pass needle up through bugle C of 9th row; 1 roc, 1 bg, 1 roc; pass needle up through bugle A of 9th row.

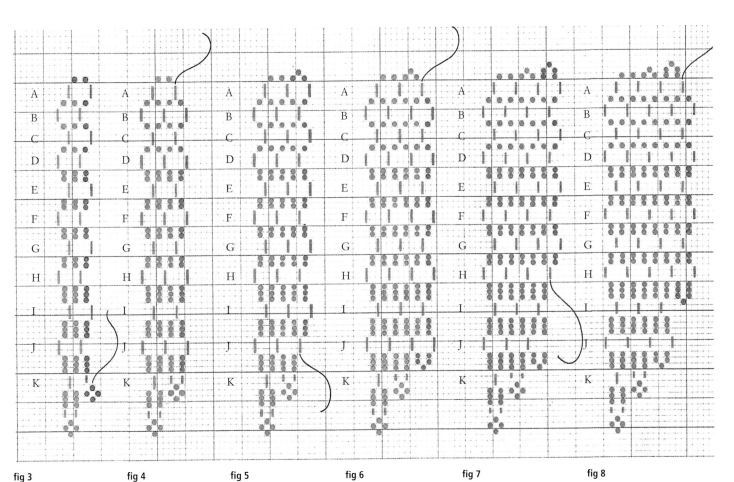

fig 3   fig 4   fig 5   fig 6   fig 7   fig 8

11th row Thread 12 roc, 1 bg, 1 roc; pass needle down through bugle B of 10th row; 1 roc, 1 bg, 1 roc; pass needle down through bugle D of 10th row; 3 roc, 1 sm bg, 4 roc. Now make a picot of last 3 beads by passing needle up through 4th last bead of this row.

12th row (fig 9) Thread 1 sm bg, 3 roc, 1 bg, 1 roc; pass needle up through bugle C of 11th row; 6 roc, 1 bg, 1 roc; pass needle over thread below bugle A of 11th row to form a loop and return needle through last bead and bugle of 12th row.

13th row Thread 3 roc; pass needle down through 2nd last bead of 12th row and pull tight to make a picot; 1 roc, 1 bg, 4 roc. Now make a picot of last 3 beads by passing needle through 4th last bead of this row; 1 bg, 1 roc; pass needle down through 5th, 6th and 7th last beads of 12th row. Make a few

fastening-off stitches around 12th row thread (fig 10), then pass needle down through rest of 12th row and cut off remainder of thread neatly.

To work left-hand side

1 Remove pin from cork board and undo knot of thread around it. Thread 1.5m (1¾yd) length which was laid to left-hand side of board and pin down middle loop of thread of beading already worked between 1st and 2nd rows, to secure it while you work.

2 Now work from right to left, that is from centre to left-hand side edge. Fig 11 shows the complete vineleaf: 1st and 2nd rows of right-hand side instructions you have just worked form the centre of the whole structure, so consider right-hand side 1st row as 2nd row for left-hand side, and work 3rd to 13th rows from centre out to left-hand edge following same threading instructions.

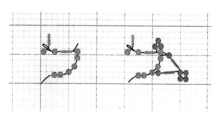

fig 10

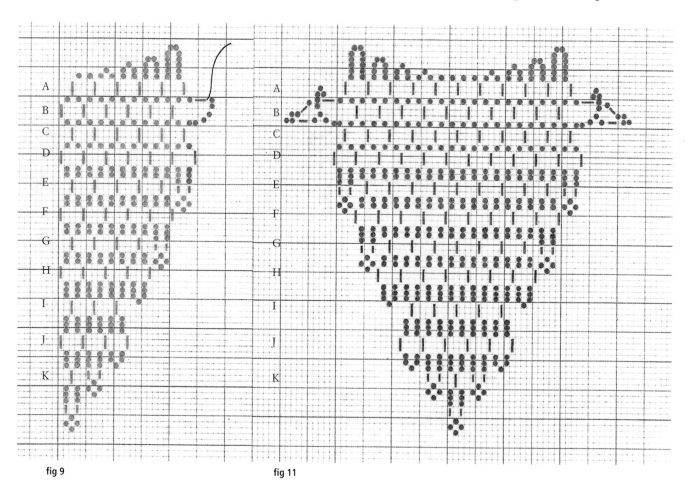

fig 9

fig 11

To work the grapes

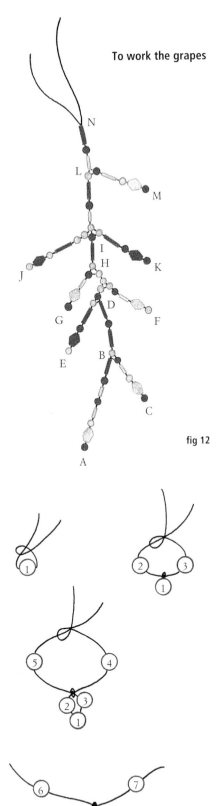

fig 12

Crystal choker grapes (fig 12) The sequence of working is from bottom grape A up to point N.

1 Cut a 75cm (30in) length of thread and thread a needle on both ends. Find the centre of the thread and, with one needle, thread on 1 purple rocaille and push down to this centre point. Thread on 1 1cm-diam pink faceted crystal next to this and take 2nd needle through this bead as well.

2 Referring to colour threading sequence in fig 12, continue to thread with both needles through same beads to point B after 1st 6mm iridescent purple bugle.

3 Using only one needle and thread, follow sequence to point C and return to point B. Using both needles and threads, thread to point D.

4 Using longest of the 2 threads, work to point F and continue in this way, always using longest of threads when you make a 'spur' off to G, K, J and M, until you reach point N.

5 Work another 'stem' of grapes in same way, tying point B between the 2 working threads at point N, giving a cluster effect to this stem.

Garnet choker grapes

1 Cut two 1m (1¼yd) lengths of thread and thread a needle on to each of the 4 ends.

2 Referring to fig 14, using one length of thread with 2 needles per branch, work 2 separate branches: one with a 9- and 17-grape bunch, and the other with a 7- and 13-grape bunch, following the

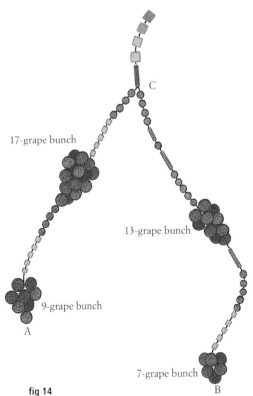

fig 14

steps shown in fig 13. The sequence of working is from A and B upwards to point C in fig 14.

3 Join the 2 branches at point C (fig 14) by threading all 4 ends through the 6mm bronze bugles and the 4 larger beads in sequence – 2 amber, 1 pinky bronze and 1 green-bronze – to blend end of grape stem in with vineleaf.

To attach grape bunches to vineleaves
Tie and knot the relevant bunches around vineleaf thread at base of bugle A in fig 1, on page 24. Thread remaining ends individually through some of the beads and bugles of the vineleaf structure and cut off neatly.

To attach beading to velvet band
Sew choker beading to velvet band by catching a row of small stitches below each bugle bead in row A.

Turn in ends of velvet ribbon and stitch on velcro fastening neatly to cover the raw ends.

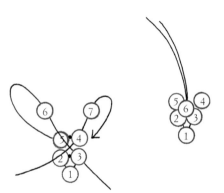

fig 13

27

Beading in the round

Having mastered the technique of beading in rows, you can move on to beading in rounds to create a circular effect. It is still easy to do, and again involves no more than a needle and thread.

Circular beading can be worked flat – to create a lace doily, for example. Alternatively, by consistently using the same number of beads in each row you can make a tubular shape, as illustrated by the bracelet on the next page. Finally, by increasing or decreasing the number of beads per round you can shape the beading to decorate shaped items, such as the perfume bottles in this chapter.

circular beading

Circular beading can be used to work some simple but very effective projects, from chokers and straps to belts and bracelets. By working in rounds rather than in rows you can create three-dimensional, tubular shapes. You can increase the length of the beading by measuring the number of rounds to a centimetre or an inch and increasing the total number of rounds accordingly. Alternatively, by using the technique of beadwrapping you can make lengths of beaded cord which will be stronger and harder-wearing.

Starting off

1 Thread a number of beads on to your working thread. Tie thread together to form a continuous circle of beads: this gives you the base or 1st round. Pass needle again through 1st bead threaded to begin working 2nd round (fig 1).

2 Work the 2nd round of beads, suspending a bead for 2nd round between a pair of beads of 1st round (fig 2).

3 Begin to work the 3rd round, taking needle and thread from the last bead threaded for 2nd round and passing it again through 1st bead threaded for 2nd round (fig 3).

4 Continue in this way (fig 4), pulling thread tight at end of each round, and work about 100 rounds, depending on length needed.

NB The bracelet seen in the photograph took 111 rounds.

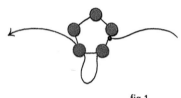

fig 1

fig 2

fig 3

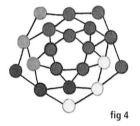

fig 4

The beading will start to form a tube after 4 or 5 rounds, and should be easy to work holding the tube between the fingers of your non-threading hand. You can slip the tube as it forms on to a pen, pencil or chopstick, depending on the diameter of the project, to use as a core to support the beading. This can be slipped out later. With practice you should find this unnecessary.

Finishing off

fig 5

You can create a simple fastening for a bracelet, for example, by following the steps outlined below. Alternatively, decorate the end of the loop with a bead drop and picot. You can make an adjustable fastening by using a short string of beads with a drop in the middle and at the end. Choose between these drops, depending on the size of your wrist.

1 Make a fastening-off stitch to form a cross between the circle of threaded beads in last round (fig 5). Attach a large bead and a small bead. Take needle back through large bead and make a fastening-off stitch. Stitch thread through beads of last few rounds. Make 2 or 3 fastening-off stitches and cut off thread neatly.

2 Put thread of other end into a needle and thread on sufficient large rocailles to make a loop which will slip over large beads of other end, then pass needle through 1st bead threaded to complete the loop.

3 Make 2 or 3 fastening-off stitches and thread through beads of last round. Cut off thread neatly.

Beadwrapping

Using the technique of beadwrapping, where beads threaded on to a continuous thread are wrapped and wound around a pre-prepared cord core, it is possible to make lengths of beaded cord. These can be worked quite quickly to make up chokers, bracelets, belts, bell pulls and many other items. So far, the techniques described have usually required careful planning and charting of beads and colours, but beadwrapping is worked to best effect with beads of one size, the chosen colours being threaded on to the working thread more or less randomly.

Making a cord core

You will need
Length of 3-strand cord
Polyester thread, colour matched to cord

Needle fine enough to pass through beads twice when threaded
Selection of similar-sized beads

To make the core
1 Carefully whip ends of cord to prevent it unravelling, by wrapping thread around ends at least 6 times (fig 1). Fasten off and cut off any excess thread.
2 Lay cord on a flat surface in a closed circle with the 2 ends butted together (fig 2).
3 Stitch these ends to the cord they are lying against, being careful not to pull too tightly. Then stitch a few times between whipping of each end. This will form a 'bridge' and make the cord circle continuous (fig 3).
NB If using the cord core for tie-backs, set the join off-centre so that when the cords are knotted together they have maximum flexibility.

fig 1

fig 2

fig 3

Wrapping the beads

1 Starting at one end of cord core, fasten on the working thread 2.5cm (1in) from end. This will form a loop from which to make a fastening for a belt, choker or bracelet, or a loop from which to hang a tie-back or a bell pull. You can vary the size of the loops depending on the fastening you are using. Thread on about 24 beads in a sequence of your choice.
2 Holding thread taut with beads pushed together, wind beaded length around cord core, pulling tightly. Holding wrapped beading firmly, stitch a few times through unwrapped cord next to beads, then pass needle through last 2 or 3 beads threaded (see position of needle in photograph).
3 Continue to thread, wind and stitch until you reach 2.5cm (1in) from other end, and fasten off neatly.
NB For ease of working, do not try to wrap too many rounds of beads before stitching through the cord.

Finishing off

1 Use a glass button with a shank and place the shank between one of the cord loops.
2 Secure by stitching through the cord, together with the shank and the other side of the cord loop.
3 Loop the other loop over this to make the fastening.

For a stylish finishing touch, try using a beautiful button in combination with simple beading. The fastening will then become the prominent feature of the design. You can be as inventive as you like, and experiment with decorative tassel fastenings or a beaded loop fastening, as appropriate.

perfume bottles

As in the grapes and vineleaves bead lace chokers on page 22, by varying the threading sequence and number of beads you can create an openwork effect, but this time working in rounds instead of rows. Depending on the shape chosen, by increasing or decreasing the number of beads per round it is possible to decorate shaped objects with beading, and this is the technique used for the perfume bottles here.

Adorned with openwork beading, one of these perfume bottles is finished with a final round of elegant teardrops, the other with beautiful crystal drops.

Teardrop perfume bottle

You will need

4m (4¼yd) polyester thread
Needle fine enough to pass through
   smallest bead twice when threaded
150 pearly blue rocailles (pbl roc)
140 sea-green rocailles (s-gr roc)
90 small yellow cut bd (sm yel cut bd)
40 large gold rocailles (lg gld roc)
40 6mm blue bugles (6m bl bg)
40 iridescent green rocailles (iri gr roc)
32 large turquoise rocailles (lg turq roc)
30 large dark blue rocailles (lg dk bl roc)
30 turquoise rocailles (turq roc)
30 small dark blue crystals (sm dk bl crs)

20 dark green rocailles (dk gr roc)
20 green rocailles (gr roc)
20 pale blue glass teardrops (ple bl tdp)
20 4mm turquoise bugles (4m turq bg)
20 small blue pearls (sm bl pl)
20 small pale blue crystals (sm ple bl crs)
10 medium blue-grey pearls
   (med bl-g pl)
10 large pale turquoise crystals
   (lg ple turq crs)
10 large pale green crystals
   (lg ple gr crs)
1 blue flat crystal (bl flt crs)
1 small pale green crystal (sm ple gr crs)

To make up

The beading is worked down from the
bottle neck. The illustration (fig 1) shows
the openwork effect you are creating.

fig 1

1st round Thread 20 lg turq roc, then tie
these around bottle neck and knot
thread so that you have a 1m (1¼yd)
end and a 3m (3¼yd) end of thread. To
prevent tangles, wind up shorter length
and tuck it into bottle ready for use
later. Now continue with longer length
threaded into needle.
2nd round Thread 1 s-gr roc between
each pair of lg turq roc of 1st round,
then pass needle again through 1st
bead of this round.
3rd round Thread 1 sm yel cut bd, 1 s-gr
roc, 1 sm yel cut bd as a picot between
each pair of s-gr roc of 2nd round, then

pass needle again through 1st and 2nd
bead of 1st picot (fig 2).
4th round Thread 1 pbl roc between

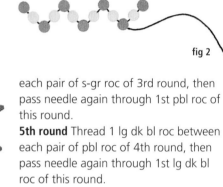

fig 2

each pair of s-gr roc of 3rd round, then
pass needle again through 1st pbl roc of
this round.
5th round Thread 1 lg dk bl roc between
each pair of pbl roc of 4th round, then
pass needle again through 1st lg dk bl
roc of this round.
6th round Thread 1 sm b pl, 1 4m turq
bg, 1 lg gld roc, 1 4m turq bg, 1 sm bl
pl into every other lg dk bl roc of 5th
round. This will make 10 loops of beads.
Then pass needle again through 1st 3
beads of 1st loop in this round (fig 3).
7th round Thread 1 pbl roc, 2 iri gr roc,
1 sm dk bl crs, 2 iri gr roc, 1 pbl roc into

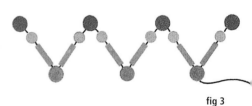

fig 3

every lg gld roc of 6th round, then pass
needle again through 1st 4 beads of
this round (fig 4).

fig 4

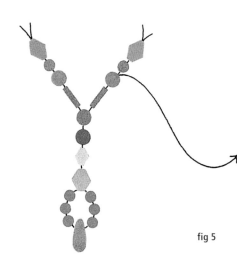

fig 5

8th round Thread 1 dk gr roc, 1 6m bl bg, 1 lg ple turq crs, 1 6m bl bg, 1 dk gr roc into every sm dk bl crs of 7th round, then pass needle again through 1st 3 beads of this round.

9th round Thread 1 pbl roc, 1 lg gld roc, 1 6m bl bg, 1 lg turq roc, 1 lg dk bl roc, 1 sm ple bl crs, 1 lg ple gr crs, 3 s-gr roc, 1 ple bl tdp, 3 s-gr roc, then pass needle back through the lg ple gr crs, sm ple bl crs, lg dk bl roc, lg turq roc, and pull up to form a drop. Then thread 1 6m bl bg, 1 lg gld roc, 1 pbl roc, and pass needle through lg ple turq crs of 8th round. Repeat this sequence between each pair of lg ple turq crs of 8th round, then pass needle again through 1st 2 beads of this round (fig 5).

10th round Thread 2 s-gr roc, 1 lg gld roc, 1 sm dk bl crs, 1 ple bl tdp, then pass needle back up through the sm dk bl crs and lg gld roc. Then thread 2 s-gr roc, and pass needle through next lg gld roc of 9th round. Repeat this sequence between each pair of lg gld roc of 9th round (fig 6).

Finish by making fastening-off stitches around working thread between beads, and passing needle through several beads before cutting off remaining thread neatly.

To work bottle neck

Rethread needle with the 1m (1¼yd) length of thread which was tucked into bottle neck and work bottle neck up:

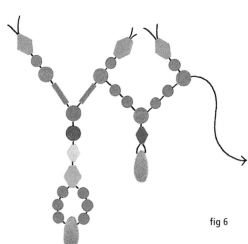

fig 6

1st round Thread 1 sm yel cut bd, 1 sm dk bl crs, 1 sm yel cut bd between every lg turq roc of bottle 1st round, then pass needle again through 1st 2 beads of this round.

2nd round Thread 1 sm ple bl crs between each pair of sm dk bl crs of 1st round, then pass needle again through 1st sm ple bl crs of this round.

3rd round Thread 1 med bl-g pl between each pair of sm ple bl crs of 2nd round, then pass needle again through 1st med bl-g pl of this round.

4th round Thread 1 s-gr roc, 1 sm yel cut bd between each pair of med bl-g pl of 3rd round, then pass needle again through 1st 2 beads of this round.

5th round Thread 1 sm dk bl crs between each pair of sm yel cut bd of 4th round, then pass needle again through 1st bead of this round.

6th round Thread 3 pbl roc between each pair of sm dk bl crs of 5th round, then pass needle again through 1st 2 beads of this round.

7th round Thread 1 pbl roc, 1 lg turq roc, 1 pbl roc between pairs of the middle 3 pbl roc of 6th round, then pass needle again through 1st 2 beads of this round.

8th round Thread 1 sm yel cut bd, 1 sm dk bl crs, 1 sm yel cut bd between each pair of lg turq roc of 7th round, then pass needle again through 1st 2 beads of this round.

9th round Thread 1 turq roc, 1 pbl roc, 1 turq roc between each pair of sm dk bl crs of 8th round, then pull up thread tightly. Finish by making fastening-off stitches around working thread between beads, and passing needle through several beads before cutting off thread.

To work bottle stopper drop

Thread 1 lg turq roc, 1 sm ple gr crs, 1 bl flt crs, 1 lg dk bl roc, 1 turq roc, then pass needle back up through 1st 4 beads to make a drop. Tie this tightly around ring of stopper and pass threads back down through the beads, before cutting off remaining thread neatly.

Crystal drop perfume bottle

You will need

4m (4¼yd) polyester thread
Needle fine enough to pass through
   smallest bead twice when threaded
145 jade rocailles (jd roc)
136 large turquoise rocailles
   (lg turq roc)
99 Delft blue rocailles (Dbl roc)
90 dark green rocailles (dk gr roc)

84 blue flat crystals (bl flt crs)
45 large dark blue rocailles (lg dk bl roc)
37 small sea-green cut beads
   (sm s-gr cut bd)
37 small dark blue crystals
   (sm dk bl crs)
18 silver metallic beads (silv met bd)
10 large blue crystals (lg bl crs)
9 large turquoise crystals (lg turq crs)

To make up

The beading is worked down from the
bottle neck.

1st round Thread 18 lg dk bl roc, then
tie these around bottle neck and knot
thread so that you have a 1m (1¼yd)
end and a 3m (3¼yd) end of thread. To
prevent tangles, wind up shorter length
and tuck it into bottle for use later.
Now continue with longer length
threaded into needle.

2nd round Thread 1 jd roc between each
pair of lg dk bl roc in 1st round, then
pass needle again through 1st bead of
this round.

3rd round Thread 1 lg turq roc between
each pair of jd roc in 2nd round, then
pass needle again through 1st bead of
this round.

4th round Thread 1 dk gr roc, 1 Dbl roc,
1 dk gr roc between each pair of lg turq
roc in 3rd round, then pass needle again
through 1st bead of this round.

5th round Thread 3 jd roc, 1 sm s-gr cut
bd, 1 lg dk bl roc, 1 sm s-gr cut bd, 3 jd
roc into every other Dbl roc of 4th

1 dk gr roc, 3 lg turq roc into every lg dk
bl roc of 5th round, then pass needle
again through 1st 6 beads of this round.

7th round Thread 1 sm s-gr cut bd, 3 jd
roc, 1 lg dk bl roc, 1 lg bl crs, 1 lg dk bl
roc, 3 jd roc, 1 sm s-gr cut bd into every
sm dk bl crs of 6th round. Pass needle
again through 1st 6 beads of this round.

8th round Thread 1 dk gr roc, 1 lg turq
roc, 2 Dbl roc, 1 lg turq crs, 2 Dbl roc, 1
lg turq roc, 1 dk gr roc into every lg bl
crs of 7th round, then pass needle again
through 1st 6 beads of this round
(fig 2).

9th round Thread 1 dk gr roc, 1 lg dk bl
roc, 1 jd roc, 1 Dbl roc, 1 jd roc, 1 lg dk
bl roc, 1 dk gr roc into every middle Dbl
roc, lg turq crs, Dbl roc of 8th round
(fig 3).

10th round Thread 1 sm dk bl crs, 3 bl flt
crs, 1 lg turq roc, then pass needle up
through 3 bl flt crs, 1 sm dk bl crs to
form a 'drop'. Work a drop each side of
the lg turq crs of 8th round and each
side of the Dbl roc of 9th round,
forming 27 drops in total (fig 4). Finish

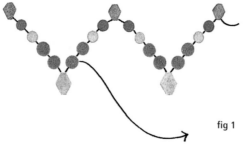

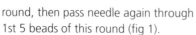

fig 1

fig 2

round, then pass needle again through
1st 5 beads of this round (fig 1).
6th round Thread 3 lg turq roc, 1 dk gr
roc, 1 Dbl roc, 1 sm dk bl crs, 1 Dbl roc,

off by making fastening-off stitches
around remaining thread and passing
needle through several beads before
cutting off remaining thread neatly.

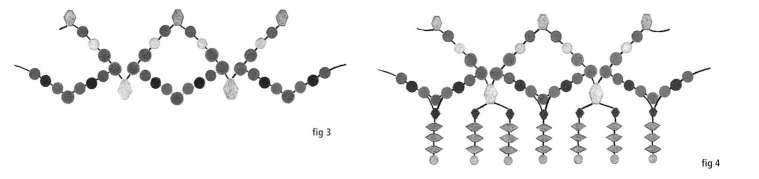

fig 3

fig 4

To work bottle neck

Rethread needle with the 1m (¼yd) length of thread which was tucked into bottle neck and work bottle neck upwards, as follows:

1st round Thread 1 lg turq roc between each pair of lg dk bl roc of 1st round of bottle beading.

2nd round Thread 1 silv met bd between each pair of lg turq roc of 1st round. Finish off thread neatly as before.

To work bottle stopper drop

Thread 1 sm s-gr cut bd, 1 lg bl crs, 1 jd roc, 1 sm dk bl crs, 3 bl flt crs, 1 lg turq roc, then pass needle back up through 1st 7 beads to make a drop. Tie this tightly around ring of stopper and pass threads back down through the beads, before cutting off thread neatly.

Bottle stopper variation

To ring the changes, you could make a small tassel drop as follows:

1 Using approximately 40cm (16in) of polyester thread, tie one end around stopper ring, leaving an 8cm (3¾in) 'tail', and thread other end into a needle. Thread on 1 large rocaille, 1 large faceted bead, 1 large rocaille.

2 Thread on 11 rocailles and pass needle up through 1st 10 rocailles threaded and large rocaille, large faceted bead, and 1st large rocaille threaded.

3 Pass needle over stopper ring and down through 1st 3 beads threaded. Thread on 11 rocailles and pass needle up through 1st 10 rocailles threaded and 1st 3 beads threaded.

4 Repeat step 3 4 times more, so that tassel has 6 individual beaded strands.

5 Pass needle again over stopper ring, and make 3 or 4 fastening-off stitches around group of threads between stopper ring and 1st large rocaille.

6 Pass needle down through 1st 3 beads threaded and cut thread off neatly.

7 Thread tail into needle and pass down through 1st 3 beads threaded and cut off neatly.

beadwrapped tie-back

Here two lengths of beadwrapping are knotted together to create an unusual, chunky, textural effect. This attractive tie-back is worked with beads of one size, threaded on to the working thread more or less at random. You could experiment with different colour themes by deciding on a dominant colour and threading more beads of this, along with occasional beads of the less dominant or highlight colour, or you could try using beads of different sizes. Bear in mind that, in the latter case, more of the cord will be revealed but you could use this to your advantage, making the cord an integral part of the design.

You can change the dimensions of the tie-back by following the calculations given here. For more information about the technique of beadwrapping see page 31.

You will need

For a tie-back 30cm (12in) approx in length:
193cm (76in) beige 3-strand cord, 5mm (¼in) in diameter
7m (7¾yd) beige polyester thread
Needle fine enough to pass through beads twice when threaded
1300 large violet rocailles (lg vio roc)
1300 large champagne rocailles (lg chm roc)
1300 large iridescent amber rocailles (lg iri amb roc)

fig 1

To make cord core

1 Cut the cord in half and then carefully whip the 4 ends by wrapping thread around ends at least 6 times. Fasten off any excess thread and cut off neatly.
2 Follow the instructions on page 31 to make 2 identical cords.

To wrap the beads

1 Starting at end of cord core, fasten on working thread 2.5cm (1in) from end. This will form a loop from which to hang the tie-back. Thread about 24 rocailles in your chosen sequence, say: 2 lg chm roc, 3 lg vio roc, 1 lg chm roc, 2 lg iri amb roc, 2 lg chm roc, 2 lg vio roc, 3 lg chm roc, 3 lg iri amb roc, 1 lg chm roc, 3 lg vio roc, 2 lg chm roc, etc.
2 Holding thread taut and with beads pushed together side by side, wind beaded length around cord core, and pull very tightly. Holding wrapped beading firmly and stitch a few times through unwrapped cord next to beads, then pass needle through last 2 or 3 beads threaded.
3 Continue to thread, wind and stitch, until you reach 2.5cm (1in) from other end of cord core, and fasten off neatly.
4 Repeat all above instructions with other length of cord core to make second tie-back.

The knot

1 Lay one length of beadwrapping on a flat surface to form a crossed loop.
2 Interlace other length with it, being careful to keep loops even. This forms a knot known as the Carrick Bend or Josephine Knot (fig 1).

To alter tie-back dimensions

If longer tie-backs are required, for instance for use with heavy velvet curtains, decide on the length and use the following formula for estimating the length of thread and number of beads required for a core made from 5mm-diameter cord.

To calculate length of thread

Allow 4cm (1½in) polyester thread for each 'wrap' around the cord
Allow 3 wraps per cm (9 wraps per in)
Length of thread required per cm (in) of cord = 4 x 3 (9 x 1½) = 12cm (13½in)
Total length of thread required = 12 (13½) x length of cord in cm (in)

To calculate number of beads

Allow 12 beads approx per wrap, using large rocailles
Allow 3 wraps per cm (9 wraps per in)
Number of beads required per cm (in) of cord = 3 x 12 (9 x 12) = 36 (108)
Total number of beads required = 36 (108) x length of cord in cm (in).

Beaded finishes

The jewel-like quality of light reflected by beaded buttons and tassels gives an extra dimension to the plainest object. We have already seen beads used as a trim on cushions, using simple needlewoven beading. This chapter contains more ideas for decorative bead finishes, from a beautiful button gracing the end of a bolster and a glorious beaded trim on a pretty drawstring bag, to glittering tassels imparting style and glamour to a velvet scarf. Finishing touches such as these are not complicated, involving no more than needle threading and a little stitching.

buttons & tassels

Handmade beaded buttons are not difficult to make and lend style to soft furnishings and a touch of originality to fashion accessories. You can either make your own buttons or decorate ready-made fabric ones. Instead of using beads you can also use sequins (for sequin button design ideas see page 104).

Decorative beaded tassels are another attractive beaded finish and make a striking addition to many accessories. To create your own tassel designs, see also page 104.

One simple way of making a beaded button is to wrap small beads over a large bead. This is the method used to make the cufflinks (see below) but you could also use it for a tassel head or to create an original finish for a cushion.

1 Using a strong polyester thread matched to beads, thread a short length through the large bead hole, pass it over outside curve of bead and back to hole

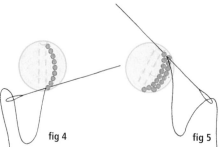

fig 1   fig 2   fig 3   fig 4   fig 5

first entered, tie ends together and knot (fig 1). Pull this loop of thread to push knot inside bead hole shaft (fig 2).
2 Thread long end of thread into a needle and pass it into the large bead hole, stitching through thread loop at top hole edge (fig 3). Thread on as

many small beads as will cover curve of large bead from top to bottom hole, say 9. Pass needle under thread loop (fig 4). Fasten off, then pass needle down through last bead threaded.
3 Thread on 2 less beads than before (7), pass over curve of large bead and through 1st bead threaded (fig 5), under thread loop, and then make a fastening-off stitch. Repeat this, alternating 9, 7, 9, 7 beads, until large bead is covered with small beads. The thread will have formed a buttonhole-type stitch around top and bottom holes (fig 6). The alternating numbers of beads will create a smooth profile.
4 Thread a bead on to working end to cover hole neatly, stitch needle through to other hole and knot short and working thread ends together. Trim off short end. Use other to attach button.

fig 6

Button cufflinks

Wrapped bead buttons can be used to make cufflinks, by joining two together with a link of beads. You can use beads which are the same size or different: in the latter case the larger button becomes the main decorative feature.

1 Make 2 buttons without the centre bead finish. Trim off short ends of threads and thread long end of one through 8 or 9 small beads. Tie this end tightly to end of thread on other button, and knot (fig 7).
2 Pass this end of thread through link of beads, so that there is an end travelling in each direction, and again tie it around other thread, by fastening-off.

3 Take end through hole (fig 8) and thread on a flat crystal and a bead, or a cup sequin (convex side uppermost) and a bead, or a bead large enough to conceal hole, then pass thread through beads to centre of bead link (fig 9).
4 Repeat with other end of thread, and tie ends together at centre of link. Thread each end in opposite directions through link (fig 10). Cut off thread.

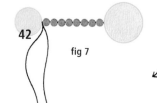

fig 7

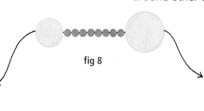

fig 8

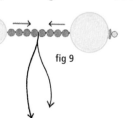

fig 9

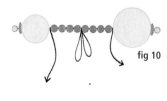

fig 10

Beaded flat buttons

To make these, you will need to use fabric-covered buttons. These can either be ready made, or you can make your own using a button-covering kit, making sure that you follow the instructions regarding the grain of the fabric carefully. When deciding what size of button to use, remember to allow for the beads or sequins which will be stitched on to it. It is possible to bead or sequin the fabric before covering the button, but although it may be a little easier to stitch this way, it can be quite tricky to keep the grain of the fabric square and avoid distorting the beading while making up the button. For ideas for sequined button designs see page 104.

1 Draw a circle on paper to same diameter as button. Starting at outside edge, lay beads side by side, with hole shafts following line of circle and leaving a small gap between them to accommodate the stitching, until there is a complete circle of beads. This is to calculate how many beads you need.

2 Using a strong polyester thread and the fabric-covered button, make a concealed fastening-on stitch (see page 15) and bring needle out half a bead width from outer edge. Make another fastening-on stitch, thread on a bead and, laying it down, pick up a little of the fabric with the needle to stitch down the bead. Do this with the other beads, spacing them carefully so that they form a continuous circle. If it is possible, draw a circle on to the fabric to follow.

3 Work out how many beads will be needed to make another circle inside outer one, and stitch as before. Repeat with more circles of decreasing diameter, until there is room to stitch only 3 beads or 1 bead in the centre. Make a fastening-off stitch, pass needle into fabric, bring it out again and cut off thread neatly.

Beaded tassels

By varying the number and sequence of beads, and using different strand lengths, you will be able to create a huge range of beautiful beaded tassels, such as those incorporated in the projects on pages 44–51. The individual strands might be designed differently, but they are usually assembled in the same way to form the finished tassel.

Make 2 strands of the tassel by threading them together as 1 string of beads, which will be tied at the centre and bent over to form the 2 strands.

1 Decide on length of strands required; then, using a strong polyester thread (or button thread if using very heavy beads) in the same colour as the beads, thread the number of beads which will equal 2 strand lengths.

2 Pinning down one end, or tying thread over last bead threaded to ensure beads do not run off thread, pass other end back through 2nd, 3rd, 4th, 5th and 6th bead at least, before making a fastening-off stitch over strand thread between 6th and 7th bead. Pass thread up through 7th and 8th bead and again fasten off. Repeat this fastening-off again if beads are heavy, pulling stitches tightly. Now pass thread through next few beads and cut off neatly. Repeat with other end of string of beads.

3 Make 5 or 6 identical strings, depending on thickness of tassel required. Lay strings side by side, and find centre point either by measuring or by bending strings in half. Double over another piece of thread and pass both ends through centre loop to form a large slip loop. Lay bunch of strings carefully into loop, until loop is at their centre points (fig 11). Then tighten loop, creating 10 or 12 strands, depending on the number of strings used.

4 To make a tassel head, slip ends of loop into a larger bead or into a wrapped bead button as described on the opposite page (fig 12).

fig 11

fig 12

beaded bolsters

Large buttons decorated with stitched beads, and with beaded tassels and drops, can be used as features in an interior design scheme. Selecting the colour of the beads to accentuate or complement other aspects of the decor can help to co-ordinate a colour scheme, add a touch of richness to enliven an otherwise bland or neutral palette, or intensify an already extravagant one. These bolsters illustrate the versatility of combining beaded accessories.

Purple damask button

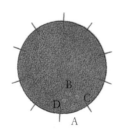

fig 1

You will need

Purple damask-covered button, 5cm (2in) diameter
Purple polyester thread
Needle fine enough to pass through beads twice when threaded
45 large royal-blue rocailles
45 large cherry-red rocailles

To make up

1 Divide circumference of button into 10 equal sections, either by marking lightly with tailor's chalk or by using pins as markers (fig 1).

2 Thread 9 large royal-blue rocailles and tie them into a circle, leaving a long and short end of thread. Knot these ends to form a not-too-tight circle of beads. Thread short end through circle of beads and cut off neatly.

3 Using long end, stitch into centre point (fig 1, point A) of one of the sections at outer edge, then pass needle in under fabric towards centre of button, coming out after about 1cm (⅜in) (point B), and catch down circle of beads by stitching over thread between two beads. Pass needle under fabric to point C and repeat, then pass under fabric to point D and repeat. Fasten off carefully, pass thread into some of the fabric and cut off neatly.

4 Repeat this sequence with a circle of 9 large royal-blue rocailles in every alternate section, and then with a circle of 9 large cherry-red rocailles in remaining sections.

Soft crimson button

You will need

Soft crimson needlecord-covered
button, 4cm (1½in) diameter
Ruby glass embroidery stone, with
metal claw mount

Crimson polyester thread
Needle fine enough to pass through
beads twice when threaded
85 large amethyst rocailles (roc)

To make up

1 Make a concealed fastening-on stitch
and bring needle out at button centre.
Stitch several times through mount.
2 Mark 5 equal sections around base of
stone and, using same length of thread,
thread on 17 roc. Pass needle through
1st 8 roc threaded and, laying circle of
beads down towards outer edge, stitch
over thread on each side of 9th/middle
bead. Pass needle under fabric 5mm
(¼in) to left side and stitch over thread

between top and bottom groups of 4
beads (fig 1). Pass needle under fabric
to right side and repeat. Pass needle
under fabric to base of stone at next pin
marker and repeat. Make 5 petal loops.

fig 1

Pale amethyst crystal loop-tassel button

You will need

Soft crimson needlecord-covered
button, 4cm (1½in) diameter
Wooden or cut cardboard washer
shape, 3cm (1¼in) diameter
Maroon, navy, green embroidery cotton
20cm (8in) maroon, navy and green
3-cord interlaced braid
Pale amethyst sewing thread

Polyester thread
Large-eyed sewing needle; straw needle
Fabric glue
3,000 2mm pale amethyst cut bugles
(cut bg)
11 large gold rocailles (roc)
2 gold Chinese-lantern-shaped beads
with large hole (Ch-ltn bd)

To make up

1 Wrap washer with embroidery cotton
and glue to button as described for the
bronze tassel-drop button opposite,
using green as main colour and navy
and maroon to mark the 6 sections.
2 Bend and stitch 3-cord braid into a
circle. Glue to outside edge of back
of washer.
3 Make 30 strings of 100 cut bg, and

fold them all in half together to make a
loop tassel. Tie thread around ends to
secure. Thread all ends through the 2
Ch-ltn bd, then divide into 6 equal
groups and, using large-eyed needle,
stitch the groups securely into inner
edge of inner hole and back of washer.
4 To finish, tie a circle of 11 roc around
point between the 2 Ch-ltn bds, thread
ends through bead circle. Cut off neatly.

Violet and cherry button

You will need

Violet needlecord-covered button,
4.5cm (1¾in) diameter
Violet polyester thread

Needle fine enough to pass through
beads twice when threaded
140 (approx) large cherry-red rocailles

To make up

1 Make a concealed fastening-on stitch
and bring out needle at outer edge. Pick
up a cherry-red rocaille and, using a
small stitch, pass needle back under
fabric, emerging a bead width away.

2 Continue stitching on rocailles at
random, leaving enough space to allow
fabric to show through.
3 Stitch beads evenly over outer rim of
button, so that there is a regular profile
of beads.

Bronze tassel-drop button

You will need

Purple damask-covered button, 5cm (2in) diameter
Wooden or cut cardboard washer shape, 3cm (1¼in) diameter
Needle fine enough to pass through beads twice when threaded
Gold, pink and green embroidery cotton
Fabric glue
Bronze polyester thread
277 large bronze rocailles (lg brz roc)
16 1cm-diam terracotta 8-grooved round beads (1cm terr 8-g bd)
10 terracotta 4-segmented pear-shaped drop beads (terr 4-seg drp bd)
2 terracotta Chinese-lantern-shaped beads (terr Ch-ltn bd)

To make up

1 Wrap gold embroidery cotton around washer shape to cover it completely. Mark 6 equal sections with pins, and decorate by wrapping 5 wraps of pink and 5 wraps of green embroidery cotton alternately at each section mark.

2 Glue completed washer centrally on to button using strong fabric glue. When completely dry, divide edge of washer into 10 sections, using pins as markers.

3 Make a concealed fastening-on stitch at a pin marker at edge of washer. Thread 5 lg brz roc, 1 1cm terr 8-g bd, 5 lg brz roc, then fasten thread at next pin marker to form a loop of threaded beads. Repeat at each pin marker to form 10 beaded loops around edge of washer. Fasten off securely.

4 Make 10 drops as follows:

1st drop Using bronze polyester thread and leaving a 20cm (8in) tail, thread 40 lg brz roc, 1 terr 4-seg drp bd, 1 lg brz roc; then pass needle up through the terr 4-seg drp bd and 40 lg brz roc, and cut off thread 20cm (8in) beyond last lg brz roc threaded. There will now be two 20cm (8in) lengths of thread to be used for stitching drop to inner edge of washer later (fig 1).

fig 1

Repeat general instructions for making 1st drop, but follow individual threading sequences below for each drop.

2nd drop Thread 15 lg brz roc, 1 1cm terr 8-g bd, 1 lg brz roc, 1 terr Ch-ltn bd, 1 1cm terr 8-g bd, 1 lg brz roc, 1 terr 4-seg drp bd, 1 lg brz roc; pass needle up through all beads threaded after last lg brz roc.

3rd drop Thread 23 lg brz roc, 1 1cm terr 8-g bd, 1 lg brz roc, 1 terr 4-seg drp bd, 1 lg brz roc; pass needle up through all beads threaded after last lg brz roc.

4th drop Thread 5 lg brz roc, 1 1cm terr 8-g bd, 9 lg brz roc, 1 Ch-ltn bd, 5 lg brz roc, 1 terr 4-seg drp bd, 1 lg brz roc; pass needle up through all beads threaded after last lg brz roc.

5th drop Thread 21 lg brz roc, 1 terr 4-seg drp bd, 1 lg brz roc; pass needle up through all beads threaded after last lg brz roc.

6th drop Thread 12 lg brz roc, 1 1cm terr 8-g bd, 1 terr 4-seg drp bd, 1 lg brz roc; pass needle up through all beads threaded after last lg brz roc.

7th drop Thread 10 lg brz roc, 1 terr 4-seg drp bd, 1 lg brz roc; pass needle up through all beads threaded after last lg brz roc.

8th & 9th drop Thread 11 lg brz roc, 1 terr 4-seg drp bd, 1 lg brz roc; pass needle up through all beads threaded after last lg brz roc.

10th drop Thread 5 lg brz roc, 1 1cm terr 8-g bd, 1 terr 4-seg drp bd, 1 lg brz roc; pass needle up through all beads threaded after last lg brz roc.

5 To finish, stitch each drop into inner edge of washer, following figs 2 to 4, taking care to space drops evenly.

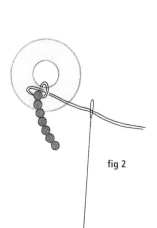

fig 2

fig 3

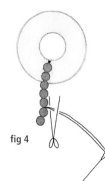

fig 4

47

evening scarf & bag

This elegant velvet scarf is finished at both ends with tassels of colourful crystals, while the bag is trimmed with a lovely netted effect.

Evening scarf

You will need

1m (1¼yd) velvet, 52cm (21in) wide
3.5m (3¾yd) polyester thread
Needle fine enough to pass through
  beads twice when threaded
360 small pale turquoise cut beads
  (sm ple turq cut bd)
260 4mm crystal bugles (4m crs bg)
240 3mm eau-de-nil bugles (3m edn bg)
160 rainbow crystals (rbw crs)
128 silver metallic rocailles (silv met roc)
20 4mm pale turquoise crystals
  (4m ple turq crs)
4 6mm turquoise crystals (6m turq crs)
2 rainbow 8-sided crystals (rbw 8sd crs)

To make up

1 With right sides together, fold velvet in half lengthways. Pin, tack and stitch down long edge to turn into tube.
2 Turn right side out and hand stitch one end closed using close gathering stitches. Pull stitches tightly together, at the same time turning under raw edge to conceal it inside tube. Secure with a few stitches across the circular finish (fig 1). Repeat with other end of tube.

To work the tassels

1 Thread 1 silv met roc, 1 4m ple turq crs, 5 silv met roc, 12 3m edn bg, 18 sm ple turq cut bd, 13 4m crs bg, 16 rbw crs, 13 4m crs bg, 18 sm ple turq cut bd, 12 3m edn bg, 5 silv met roc, 1 4m ple turq crs, 1 silv met roc. Fasten off at each end.
2 Work 9 more of these strings and separate them into 2 bunches of 5.
3 Lay down a bunch of 5 strings and follow instructions on page 43 (fig 11).
4 Thread 2 ends of noose thread through 1 silv met roc, 1 6m turq crs, 1 silv met roc, 1 rbw 8sd crs, 1 silv met roc, 1 6m turq crs 1 silv met roc. Attach to centre of circular finish. Repeat with other end.

fig 1

Evening bag

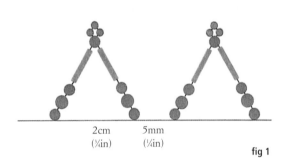

2cm   5mm
(¾in)   (¼in)

fig 1

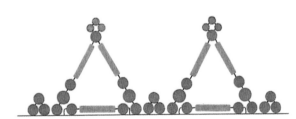

fig 2

You will need

Velvet drawstring bag, 65cm (25½in) in circumference
5m (5½yd) approx polyester thread
5m (5½yd) approx crochet cotton
Needle fine enough to pass through smallest bead twice when threaded
600 2mm green-bronze cut bugles (2m gr-brz cut bg)
537 green-bronze cut beads (gr-brz cut bd)

To make up

1 Open out bag to smooth out drawstring gathers. At a side seam, make a concealed fastening-on stitch, then thread 1 ptl-gr roc, 1 lg s-gr roc, 1 ptl-gr roc, 1 6m iri gr-gld bg, 1 ptl-gr roc, 3 gr-brz cut bd; pass needle down through ptl-gr roc to form a picot of the 3 gr-brz cut bd, then thread 1 6m iri gr-gld bg, 1 ptl-gr roc, 1 lg s-gr roc, 1 ptl-gr roc.
2 Make a fastening-off stitch 2cm (¾in) along top edge and pass needle 5mm (¼in) along, sewing invisibly through folded fabric of top. Make a fastening-on stitch and repeat threading sequence (fig 1).
3 Continue by beading around top of bag, until you have completed 26 repeats in total, then between 1st and last repeat 5mm (¼in) gap, make a picot with 3 ptl-gr roc, passing needle invisibly through fabric fold to come out close to 1st ptl-gr roc of next repeat, thread 1 ptl-gr roc, 1 6m iri gr-gld bg, 1 ptl-gr roc, passing needle down into fabric fold, then repeat this sequence until you have completed each repeat (fig 2).

To work netting

1 Using a needle threaded with crochet cotton, make a concealed fastening-on stitch and bring needle out to right side of bottom line of drawstring casing stitching, next to a side seamline.
2 Thread 1 lg brz-gr roc, 1 lg gr s-b ob bd, 1 lg brz-gr roc, and stitch into casing seamline 2.5cm (1in) along. Making a loop hanging 1cm (⅜in) approx from casing seamline, make a fastening-off stitch, bring needle back to right side of fabric close to the same point, and repeat this sequence until you reach 1st loop again (fig 3).
NB The casing is 55cm (22in) in circumference, and takes 22 repeats of loops; if your bag is a different size, adjust number of repeats as necessary.
3 Make a fastening-off stitch at beginning of 1st loop, and carefully stitch through 1st half of loop thread to secure (fig 4 opposite).
4 Take needle through 1st and 2nd bead on loop to begin to thread 2nd round. Allowing 3.5cm (1⅜in) of crochet cotton per loop, multiply this by number of loops, and tie a contrasting colour of thread at this measurement along the next length of cotton you are using, so that when you reach end of 2nd round you can make sure your last fastening-off stitch is at this point, then stitch through cotton again to begin 3rd round (fig 5 opposite).
5 Repeat instructions from steps 1–4 to work 4th and 5th round. Stitch through cotton and knot at middle of ending loop, which will be concealed by middle

267 6mm iridescent green-gold bugles (6m iri gr-gld bg)
220 large bronze-green rocailles (lg brz-gr roc)
133 large sea-green rocailles (lg s-gr roc)
114 petrol-green rocailles (ptl-gr roc)
110 large green sand-blasted oblate beads (lg gr s-b ob bd)
9 5mm-diam dark green crystals (5m dk gr crs)

fig 3

fig 4

fig 5

bead. As long as you have the same length of cotton for each round, a gentle shake will allow the beads to settle into loops of equal depth when all rounds are completed.

To work tassel finish

1 Fasten a strong piece of crochet cotton, same colour as velvet, to middle of bag base and, squeezing base tightly, begin to wrap cotton around folds of fabric, decreasing in tightness as you wrap upwards, stopping and finishing off at 3cm (1¼in) approx. This will form the beaded base above tassel (fig 6).

2 Measure 12 equal sections around wrapped base at widest point and mark with pins.

3 Using polyester thread, thread 1 6m iri gr-gld bg, 1 ptl-gr roc, 1 6m iri gr-gld bg, 1 ptl-gr roc, 3 gr-brz cut bd, pass needle back through the ptl-gr roc to form a picot of the cut beads, then thread 1 6m iri gr-gld bg, 1 ptl-gr roc, 1 6m iri gr-gld bg, stitch into base securely and pass needle back up through last bugle. Treating this as 1st bugle of previous sequence, continue until you have worked 12 beaded 'points' (fig 7), which will form a flower-petal effect around base finish.

4 Between each of the 'points' stitch a picot of ptl-gr roc, and below these a round of vertical 6m iri gr-gld bg, to form a band (fig 8).

5 Continue to stitch rounds of ptl-gr roc picots, which will decrease in size to middle of bag base, and finish off neatly and securely.

6 Following basic beaded tassel instructions on page 43, make a 20-strand tassel of 30 2m gr-brz cut bg, ending with 15 gr-brz cut bd.

7 To make tassel head, thread on 1 ptl-gr roc, 1 5m dk gr crs, 1 ptl-gr roc, 1 lg s-gr roc, and stitch into end of beaded base. Make several fastening-off stitches into beaded base and cut off neatly.

To work drawstring cord finish

1 Gather velvet finish at the ends and stitch on 3 5m dk gr crs, with a beaded picot of ptl-gr roc inbetween them (fig 9).

2 From centre of crystals, thread 1 lg s-gr roc, 3 ptl-gr roc, 1 5m dk gr crs, 1 ptl-gr roc, 3 gr-brz cut bd, then pass needle up through the ptl-gr roc to form a picot of the cut beads. Pass your thread through all other beads, and then finish off neatly and securely between the crystals.

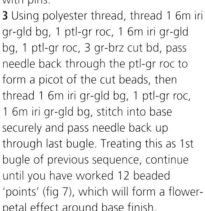

fig 6

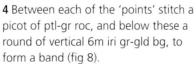

fig 9

fig 7

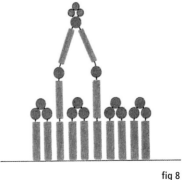

fig 8

beaded bags

Beads can add a pretty, personal touch to ready-made bags, such as the useful drawstring versions seen here. The plaid bag is finished with a stunning colourful trim worked in lime-green and yellow beads, while the rich velvet ruby bag has a glittering garnet and gold trim.

Beaded ends for the drawstring cords themselves add the final stylish finish.

Ruby bag

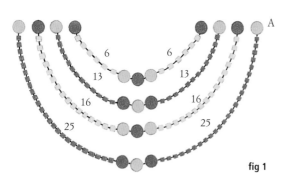

fig 1

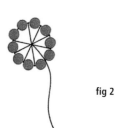

fig 2

You will need

Velvet drawstring bag, 64cm (25in) in circumference

4.5m (4¾yd) approx polyester thread, colour matched to velvet

Needle fine enough to pass through smallest bead twice when threaded

To make up

1 Open out bag to smooth out drawstring gathers. Starting at one side seamline and using a concealed fastening-on stitch, bring needle out under bottom drawstring casing seamline on right side.

2 Thread 1 lg iri gld roc, 25 sm gnt cut bd, 1 lg iri gnt roc, 1 lg iri gld roc, 25 sm gnt cut bd, 1 lg iri gld roc.

3 Measuring 6.5cm (2½in) along gather line, pass needle through to reverse side and make a fastening-off stitch, pass needle back towards fastening-on stitch by 5mm (¼in) and bring it through to right side.

4 Thread 1 lg iri gnt roc, 16 sm yel cut bd, 1 lg iri gld roc, 1 lg iri gnt roc, 16 sm yel cut bd, 1 lg iri gnt roc, and pass through to reverse side 5mm (¼in) from fastening-on stitch. Make a fastening-off stitch and bring needle through to right side of fabric 5mm (¼in) to right of last stitch.

5 Thread 1 lg iri gld roc, 13 sm yel cut bd, 1 lg iri gnt roc, 1 lg iri gld roc, 1 lg iri gnt roc, 13 sm yel cut bd, 1 lg iri gnt roc, and stitch through to reverse side 5mm (¼in) from last stitch. Make a fastening-off stitch and bring needle through to right side.

888 small garnet cut beads (sm gnt cut bd)

544 small yellow cut beads (sm yel cut bd)

144 large iridescent garnet rocailles (lg iri gnt roc)

104 large iridescent gold rocailles (lg iri gld roc)

6 Thread 1 lg iri gnt roc, 6 sm yel cut bd, 1 lg iri gld roc, 1 lg iri gnt roc, 1 lg iri gld roc, 6 sm yel cut bd, 1 lg iri gnt roc. Pass needle through to reverse side 5mm (¼in) from last stitch, make a few fastening-off stitches and cut off thread neatly (fig 1).

7 Starting again with a concealed fastening-on stitch at point A, repeat the sequence. Continue in this way around gather line until you have completed 10 repeats in total.

To finish

1 Pull drawstring cords to make them equal in length, and bind the pieces of cord together for each pull by whipping ends together as for the plaid bag (see fig 3 opposite), cutting off remaining cord neatly.

2 Make a large knot in the thread, then pass needle up through base of one of cord ends, and out through top of whipping. Thread 10 lg iri gnt roc and wrap them around cord, stitching through to anchor them. Bring needle out just below this round, thread another 10 lg iri gnt roc and repeat, then 2 more rounds of 10 lg iri gnt roc, making 4 rounds including 1st. Stitch across last round, and bring thread out of centre point (fig 2).

3 Thread 20 sm gnt cut bd, 1 lg iri gld roc, 20 sm gnt cut bd, and stitch through base to make a loop. Thread 18 sm yel cut bd, 1 lg iri gnt roc, 18 sm yel cut bd, and stitch through base to make a loop. Thread 12 sm gnt cut bd, 1 lg iri gld roc, 12 sm gnt cut bd, and again make a loop; thread 8 sm yel cut bd, 1 lg iri gnt roc, 8 sm yel cut bd, and make another loop. This will form 4 loops, graduated in size (fig 3).

fig 3

Plaid bag

You will need

Plaid drawstring bag, 164.5cm (65in) in circumference
2.5m (2¾yd) polyester thread
Needle fine enough to pass through beads twice when threaded

428 lime-green rocailles (lim-gr roc)
84 large matt yellow rocailles (lg mt yel roc)
30 large purple sand-blasted oblate beads (lg pur s-b ob bd)

To make up

1 Open out bag to smooth out drawstring gathers. Make a concealed fastening-on stitch: pass needle between turned-over fabric of top edge, from drawstring gathering line to top edge. Hold a tail of thread at drawstring line and make a few fastening-on stitches, ensuring that they are secure, and then pull thread tail a little and cut it off, so that tail slips invisibly into fabric fold (fig 1).

2 Using this secured thread, thread 1 lim-gr roc, 1 lg mt yel roc, 1 lg pur s-b ob bd, 1 lg mt yel roc, 6 lim-gr roc, 1 lg mt yel roc, 6 lim-gr roc, then pass needle up through 1st 4 beads threaded, make

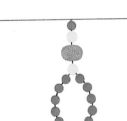

fig 1

To finish

1 Pull drawstring cords to make them equal in length, and bind the pieces of cord together for each of the 2 pulls by whipping ends together, cutting off remaining cord neatly (fig 3).
2 Make a large knot in the thread and pass needle up through base of one of

fig 3

cord ends and out through top of whipping. Thread 4 lim-gr roc and pass needle back up through base.
3 Repeat this sequence 7 times more to form a beaded end, then from centre of base thread 1 lg pur s-b ob bd, then the beaded loop sequence as for top edge (fig 4).
4 Finish off thread securely, and repeat for the other cord pull.

fig 2

a fastening-off stitch, and advance needle and thread invisibly 6cm (2½in) through fabric fold, make another fastening-off stitch. Repeat the sequence to make a loop (fig 2).
3 Continue in this way every 6cm (2½in) around top of bag, until you have 26 beaded loops.
NB The 2 bags used here both have plain cord endings. If the bag you are working on has a fabric tag attached, you can follow the instructions for the drawstring cord finish as for the evening bag seen in the photograph on page 51.

fig 4

fringing

This is one of the simplest needle-threading techniques, and is a classic method exemplified in 'Tiffany' style lampshades and the dresses of the 1920s 'flappers', where the movement of the Charleston dance made the bead-fringed dresses shimmer in the light. The threading may be comparatively simple, but this technique creates a beautiful effect, especially when used as a shade, curtain or blind edging, with light shining through the different qualities and colours of glass in the various beads.

Starting off

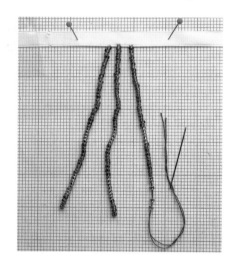

Beaded fringing can be worked by attaching each string of beads either directly to the object to be decorated or to a narrow tape or ribbon, which is then itself applied to the object. If the fringing is to be worked on to a length of tape or ribbon, it is helpful to pin this to your cork board, moving the fringed length along as it is finished and re-pinning the next section to be worked, repeating this until the required length is completed. Whatever base the fringe is to be worked on to, the fringing techniques are the same. There are two main methods.

Making a long fringe

Here, the strings of beads are attached individually to form the fringe. Generally, this method would be used when working a long fringe; it is also the best method to use when applying a fringe to static objects, as opposed to clothing and accessories.

Ensuring the bead diameter is large enough to accommodate 4 thicknesses of polyester thread, work as follows:
1 Allow 15cm (6in) approx of thread over expected length of finished string, and double that measurement.
So, for a 20cm (8in) string:
(20cm/8in + 15cm/6in) x 2 = 70cm (28in) thread required
2 Double the thread and thread both ends into a needle. Sew ends through fringe base and through loop where thread is doubled, and pull tight (fig 1).

3 Thread on required number of beads, and pass needle back up through 2nd last bead threaded, so that last bead forms end anchor. Make a fastening-off stitch with both threads between 2nd and 3rd last beads (figs 2, 3 and 4).
4 Pass needle up to between 3rd and 4th last beads, and repeat fastening-off stitch.
5 Repeat this 2 or 3 times more, pulling fastening-off stitch tightly each time, and ensuring string of beads is hanging smoothly, not too tightly, and not so loosely that there is thread showing anywhere. To finish, tug the string of beads gently to ensure fastening-off is secure, and cut off remaining thread ends neatly (fig 5).
6 Move to next point to be fringed, and repeat process until entire length of fringe is completed.

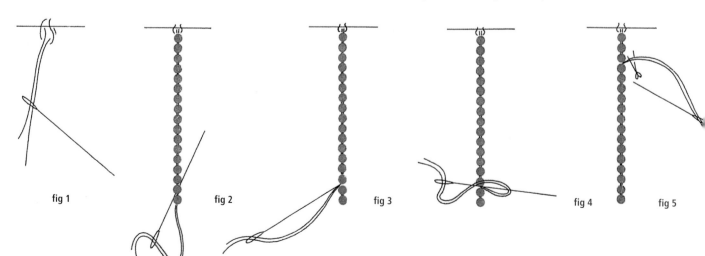

fig 1   fig 2   fig 3   fig 4   fig 5

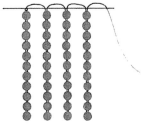

fig 7

Making a short fringe

Here, the fringe is worked with one continuous thread through all the strings of beads (fig 6). This method is used when working a shorter length of fringe, as it is easier to keep the strings smooth and the beads hanging straight when passing the needle back up through a shorter length. Use it also when the bead diameter will only accommodate 2 thicknesses of thread. It is generally the best method to use for fringing applied to clothing or accessories, as here in the shot-gauze fringed bag, since there is no risk of the fastening-off stitches working loose with the movement of the fabric when worn, as they may do with the first method.

However, there are no hard-and-fast rules, so do experiment.

The bag in the photograph was fringed using 49 strings of beads and bugles and approximately 5m (5¼yd) of polyester thread.

1 To calculate quantity of thread needed, double length of each string and add one-third of total to allow for fastening-on and off.

2 When fringing a short width, double thread quantity and tie it at centre of fringed base.

3 Thread one end and work fringing from middle to side.

4 Thread other end and work whole length of thread for each string. Continue until fringing is complete.

You will find further ideas and instructions for designing and charting beaded fringing on page 106. It is also possible to create waved and other unusual profiles to the bottom edge of the fringe, so do experiment with this interesting design possibility.

Fringed bag

1 Pin the bag to a corkboard, and divide bottom edge into 8 equal sections, marked with pins.

2 Pass threaded needle through bottom of bag at point A, leaving a short tail. Tie tail and working length together. The tail can either be threaded down 1st string of beads or stitched neatly into side seam when fringing is completed.

3 Working left to right from threading sequence chart (fig 7), thread on 2 iridescent green rocailles, 1 gold rocaille, 1 iridescent green rocaille, 1 leaf-green rocaille, 1 iridescent green rocaille, 1 leaf-green bugle, 1 leaf-green rocaille, 1 iridescent green rocaille, 1 gold rocaille and pass needle up through all rocailles threaded above last gold rocaille.

4 Continue threading and work to middle of chart (B) and from point B to D, making sure that all strings are equally spaced.

5 Repeat from A to C 3 more times between other pin points, remembering to add last string D at last pin point.

6 Pull thread firmly but not too tightly, as strings of beads and bugles should be fluid, not stiff.

NB It may be necessary to use more than one length of thread if width to be fringed is quite extensive.

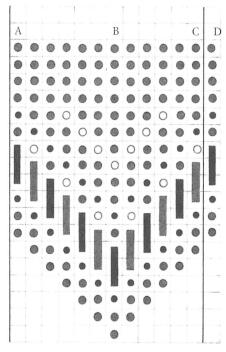

fig 8

lampshade cover

The beauty of fringing, whether worked in an intricate or a simple design, lies in the rich waterfall effect of beads hanging either closely side by side, or spaced as a fringe of long drops as in this lovely lampshade cover. Changing the colour of the light bulb used in the lamp would enable you to transform the overall effect.

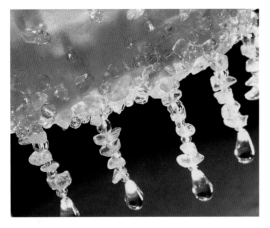

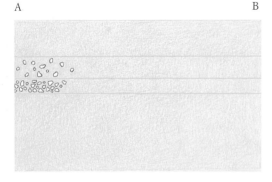

A   B

C   D

fig 1

You will need

Cream parchment lampshade,
   85cm (34in) circumference x 14cm
   (5½in) deep
25cm (10in) cream organza,
   115cm (45in) wide
25cm (10in) pale yellow silk dupion slub,
   115cm (45in) wide
Embroidery hoop or frame (optional)
Transparent nylon thread
Fine straw or beading needle
Pale yellow sewing thread
Sewing needle
500 polished drilled rock crystals (rk crs)
350 4mm-diam clear glass
   faceted beads (4m fc bd)
75 6mm-diam clear glass
   faceted beads (6m fc bd)
35 clear glass pear-shaped drop bead
   (drp bd)

To prepare fabric

1 With right sides together, pin pale yellow dupion slub to cream organza, then tack and machine stitch along one long edge. Press seam flat, and pink raw edges with pinking shears.
2 Open out joined fabrics right side up, and on cream organza mark 15cm (6in) from each edge, leaving a middle section of 85cm (34in), which will be the length to be beaded. Measure up 2cm (⅝in) from joining seam and make a tacking line across width of organza – this is where the dense beading will be. Then from that line measure up 3cm (1¼in) and again make a tacking line across width of organza – this is where the lighter beading will be (fig 1).

To work beading

1 Stretch joined fabric into a rectangular embroidery frame, or work sections along the width with organza part-mounted in a circular embroidery hoop, or carefully work the beading with fabric unstretched. If using a frame or hoop, make sure you keep grain (thread lines) of fabric straight to prevent it becoming distorted, which in turn will cause beading to be distorted when finished.
2 Begin by working 2cm (⅝in) border of dense beading. For every 10cm (4in) length, you will need 5 6m and 20 4m fd bd. Using the thread doubled, sew on beads randomly but evenly, filling in-between spaces with rk crs. Secure each of these with 2 stitches – one on either side – to keep it flat.
3 When dense beading is complete, work 3cm (1¼in) band of lighter beading. For every 10cm (4in) length, you will need 5 4m fc bd and approx 10 rk crs (as these are a natural stone the size varies, so use artistic discretion). Stitch on beads so that they appear to be lightly scattered on to the fabric. As thread is transparent, you can take it from bead to bead on reverse of fabric without finishing off each time.

To work fringing

1 Using a pencil, mark lightly every 2.5cm (1in) along seamline below dense beading area.
2 Count out beads for the fringing: for each fringe you will need 4 rk crs, 1 6m fc bd and 4 4m fc bd, and 1 drp bd.
3 Make 1 or 2 fastening-on stitches to fasten thread to 1st pencil mark. Thread 1 rk crs, 1 6m fc bd, 1 rk crs, 1 4m fc bd, 1 rk crs, 1 4m fc bd, 1 rk crs, 1 4m fc bd, 1 rk crs, 1 4m fc bd, 1 drp bd. Pass needle up through all beads and secure with 2 or 3 fastening-off stitches; then pass thread along back of fabric to next mark, and repeat with all fringes.

fig 2

To make up

1 With right sides together, fold points A and B over to points C and D, then pin, tack and machine sew with a 2cm (⅝in) seam allowance. Turn right side out and press down top seam. Make this 'tube' into a circle: either machine stitch sides together and press seam open, or turn in edges, butt together and stitch to join invisibly (fig 2).

2 Mark a line 7.5cm (3in) from top edge, by pinning around the circumference, and hand stitch a gathering thread along this line. Slip completed cover over cream parchment shade and draw up gathers to fit top edge, ensuring that bottom edges of beaded cover and shade cover are lying together. Secure with 1 or 2 fastening-off stitches.

3 Punching needle carefully through parchment at approx 3cm (1¼in) intervals, sew beaded cover to shade.

59

Pin & wire beading

Pin beading involves using beads and/or sequins, and pins. It dates from the eighteenth and early nineteenth centuries, when pin-beaded pincushions or pinpillows were made to give as tokens of friendships and love. The cushions were tightly filled with sawdust or bran to provide a firm anchor for the pins. Today, the availability of compressed cushions and polystyrene shapes means you can easily pin bead little gifts or Christmas tree decorations, such as the baubles in this chapter.

Wire beading is the art of threading beads on to wire, then twisting them to create elegant shapes, like the colourful flowers and beautiful butterflies seen in this chapter. The craft is believed to date from as early as the fifteenth century and became particularly popular in Victorian England.

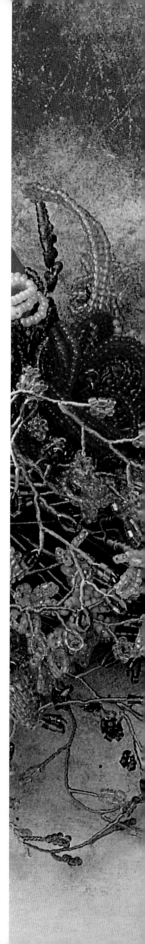

pin & wire beading

Pin-beaded patterns are suitable for small decorations such as glittering baubles and other festive decorations, while wire beading is ideal for creating naturalistic designs, such as those seen on pages 72–75, for example. The skill lies in the manipulation of the wired beads to create the required form. You might find it useful to follow a photograph or illustration – even perhaps real flowers – for reference.

Starting pin beading

In this technique, the beads and sequins are pinned into densely compressed cotton or polystyrene shapes or balls, using 'lill' pins – short pins, 14mm (½in) long. If the base shape used is large it is possible to use ordinary dressmaking pins, but with smaller shapes you will need to use lill pins so that they do not cross over each other inside the base shape, making it difficult to push more in.

Unless you wish to paint the surface of the ball or cover it with fabric, it is best to pin closely to cover the surface completely. Depending on the desired effect, use beads only (fig 1), sequins only (fig 2), or both on one pin (fig 3). You can choose any combination of these, but if you choose beads only you may need to colour the surface of the ball first in a complementary colour. Cup sequins, pinned concave side down, give a pleasing, smooth profile to the finished work.

When designing for a ball shape, it might be helpful to draw out the ball on paper as an exploded shape – very like a flat representation of the world in an atlas. If this is drawn to scale, it can be glued to the ball and the design pinned through this into the ball, enabling you to work more complicated designs.

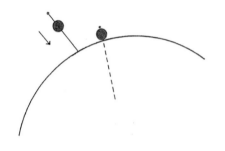

fig 1

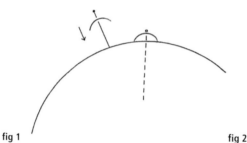

fig 2

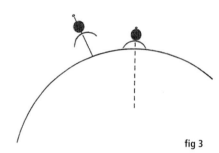

fig 3

Pin-beaded Christmas pudding

When working pin beading, hold the bead shape either in one hand while you work the pinning with the other, or, if you prefer to have both hands free, scrunch up some tissue paper to make a 'nest' in which to rest the shape, turning it as you work.
It is best to pin in the colour that is to be least dominant – the background colour – first and then pin shape outlines overlapping this, to give a definite line to the design. This will enable you to create different intensities and subtleness of colour.

1 Choose cup sequins which match as closely as possible the natural colours of the pudding. Use a small compressed cotton ball for the shape.
2 Draw the design on to the ball using a felt-tip pen.
3 Pin top of pudding shape using mother-of-pearl cup sequins, inserted very close together and pinned concave side down.

4 Pin fruit using dark brown cup sequins, interspersed with 'mixed peel' and 'cherries' using orange, bronze and red cup sequins.
5 Finish by adding a small looped bow, decorated with sequin leaves and red beads to give a holly-berry effect, attached by 2 dressmaking pins. If you insert the pins at an angle they will not pull out when the ball is suspended.

Starting wire beading

This technique basically consists of threading beads on to fine wire and twisting the wire to secure the beads.

Materials suitable for wire beading include silver- or gold-coloured electrical, craft or beading wires. Angling shops are another good source, as they sell many different colours of fine wire which are used by fishermen to tie fishing flies. The wire might seem attractive enough to leave unwrapped, but the traditional finish to a flower stem is to wrap it with green silk floss. With a little practice this process can be completed quite quickly, and is useful if the bead flower is attached to a stem made of thicker wire, as the join will be disguised.

Experiment by varying the different sizes and colour combinations of the beads in order to achieve a realistic effect, or work entirely from your intuition and imagination, and see what you can create.

Wire beaded flower

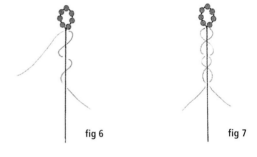

Choose beads to match the colours of your chosen design. Use either solid or transparent rocailles to vary the effect. Use bugles or rocailles for the stamens and green silk floss for covering the wire stem.

1 Take 30cm (12 in) of wire. Bend in half and thread 9 rocailles on to one end of wire. Push up to the bend.

2 Twist wire together, below loop of beads (fig 1). Thread on another 9 rocailles on one end and twist together (fig 2).

3 On the other end thread on 9 rocailles and twist again (fig 3). Repeat again with each end (fig 4). When you have 5 petals, twist ends securely together. Take one end of the wire and pass it through the petals to the centre of the flower.

4 Thread on one yellow rocaille to form stamen in the middle of the flower (fig 5).

5 Push end of wire back down to join other end and twist together.

6 Cover wire stem by wrapping with green silk floss (figs 6 and 7).

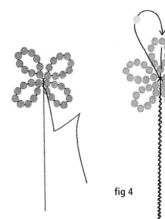

Making a bouquet

To create a bouquet effect you could make several flowers, and wire them all together as a bunch, varying the length of the stems as if arranging a real bouquet. Tying them with a decorative ribbon, finished with a bow covering the wiring, would complete the final arrangement.

embellished tassels

Wire-beading is a versatile technique which you can apply to many different facets of home decoration. These wire-beaded flowers make gorgeously decorative tassels and tie-backs that will enhance any home.

Gold roses and pearls

fig 1

fig 2

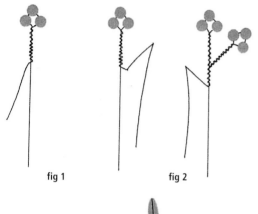

fig 3

You will need

Pink silky tassel, 12cm (5in) long approx
7 gold fabric roses
Reel fine wire
Gold spray craft paint
Cork board and plastic sheet
100 (approx) pearl oats
50 (approx) round pearls, 3mm and 6mm diameter

To make up

1 To assemble sprays of wired round pearls, cut a piece of wire 40cm (16in) long approx and bend it in half. Thread on 3 3mm round pearls, push up to the bend and twist wire several times below them, forming a picot (fig 1).

2 Take one end of wire and bend approx 2cm (¾in). Thread on 3 more 3mm round pearls and push up to this point, then twist to join main stem. Twist stem together several times (fig 2).

3 Using longer length of wire, repeat sequence with another 3 3mm round pearls. Continue in this way, varying length of side branches.

4 Repeat steps 1–3 to make another spray, but using only single pearl oats (fig 3).

5 Make several more sprays, varying finished lengths, and incorporating some 6mm round pearls with the 3mm round pearls.

6 Push finished sprays into a cork board protected with a plastic sheet, and spray with gold craft paint.

7 When dry, push each spray into base of tassel head, bend back to stem, twist to secure. Work all round base of tassel head, alternating lengths of sprays.

8 To finish, glue 7 fabric roses evenly around base of tassel head, concealing where sprays are attached.

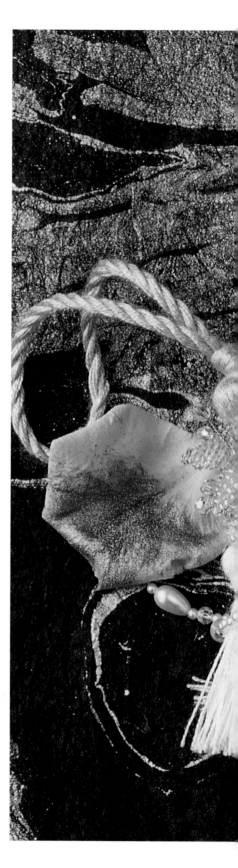

Pearl and crystal flowers

You will need

Cream tassel, 15cm (6in) circumference
    at base of tassel head
Reel fine gold-coloured wire
Cream polyester thread
Sewing needle
500 2mm rainbow crystal cut
    bugles (2m rbw crs bg)

250 2mm-diam round pearls (2m rnd pl)
20 6mm pearl oats (6m prl oat)
20 3mm rainbow crystal cut bugles
    (3m rbw crs bg)
8 4mm-diam rainbow faceted crystals
    (4m rbw fc crs)
7 1cm-diam round pearls (1cm rnd prl)
7 7mm-diam round pearls (7m rnd prl)

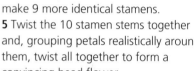

To make up pearl flower

1 For each flower petal, carefully cut a
piece of wire 40cm (16in) long. Bend in
half and thread on 3 2m rnd prl. Bend
to form a picot and pass right-hand end
of wire through 1st 2 pearls threaded
(fig 1).

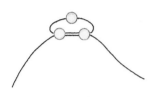

fig 1

fig 2

2 Pull these close together, thread 3 2m
rnd prl on to left-hand end of wire and
bend towards right side (fig 2).
3 Pass right-hand end of wire through
pearls towards left side. Repeat
sequence with a row of 4 and then 5
2m rnd pl, then decrease using 4, then
3, then 2, then 1, to complete the petal
(fig 3). Make 4 more petals identically.
4 To make the stamens, cut a piece of
wire 15cm (6in) long approx, bend it in
half, thread on a 6m prl oat and twist
wire for about 2cm (¾in) to form the

fig 3

stamen. Repeat these instructions to
make 9 more identical stamens.
5 Twist the 10 stamen stems together
and, grouping petals realistically around
them, twist all together to form a
convincing bead flower.

To make up crystal flowers

1 Make 20 petals as for pearl flower,
but using 2m rbw crs bg instead of 2m
rnd prl.
2 Make 20 stamens using a single 3m
rbw crs bg, and 8 stamens using a
single 4m rbw fc crs.
3 Assemble 3 flowers, 2 with 5 petals
and 10 3m rbw crs bg stamens, and 1
with 10 petals and 8 4m rbw fc crs
stamens. Group all 5 flowers together
so that the large crystal flower hangs
below the 2 pearl flowers, with a crystal
flower to either side of pearl flowers,
and twist stems together to form a
spray of flowers.
4 Using cream polyester thread stitch 7
1cm rnd prl and 7 7m rnd prl alternately
around base of tassel head. Position
spray of flowers above this row of pearls
and stitch securely into tassel head.
Bend petals out gently.

Old roses and pearls

You will need

Large soft pink tassel tie-back,
    25cm (10in) circumference at base of
    tassel head
6 old rose paper roses with paper
    leaves, 3.5cm (1½in) diameter

Fabric glue
Soft pink strong thread
Sewing needle
16 4mm-diam pale pink round pearls
12 5mm-diam pale pink round pearls
7 1cm-diam round pearls

To make up

1 Using soft pink strong thread, stitch
pearls to tassel head in order to create a
random scattered effect, alternating
bead sizes.

2 Pin paper roses around base of tassel
head, spacing them evenly to create a
natural effect.
3 Attach roses to tassel head securely
using fabric glue.

Gold bow and pearls

You will need

Large cream cotton tassel tie-back, 30cm (12in) circumference at base of tassel head
Reel fine gold-coloured wire
Cream polyester thread; sewing needle
1 pearl and 2 crystal 5-petalled flowers, made as for pearl and crystal flowers

To make up

1 Make 10 tiny tassels using soft pink embroidery cotton, by making equal bundles of 5cm (2in) lengths and tying them at their centres. Bend each bundle in half, smooth down and wrap more soft pink embroidery cotton around the bunch 5mm (¼in) from centre tie.
2 Stitch 5 fabric flowers around tassel head and stitch completed tassel to end of one of main tassel strands. Repeat with other 9 tiny tassels, dotting them among the strands evenly, or stitching a strand into a loop and attaching a tiny tassel to the loop end.

Rainbow crystals and pearls

You will need

Small cream tassel 10cm (4in) approx long, encircled by 8 smaller tassels
305 2mm rainbow crystal cut bugles
120 3mm-diam round pearls

To make up

1 Make 5 petals as for the pearl and crystal flowers, using 2mm rainbow crystal cut bugles.
2 Make 5 larger petals, using 36 bugles instead of 25.
3 Make 8 stamens using 4mm-diam rainbow faceted crystals, and 6 stamens using a single crystal rocaille for each.
4 Assemble the flower by grouping the 5 smaller petals around the bunch of stamens, and the 5 larger petals around the smaller petals. Twist all stems together and cut so that only 1cm (⅜in) of main stem remains. Push this into tassel head and stitch to secure.
5 Using 2 rainbow faceted crystals and 9 3mm-diam round pearls per drop in sequence shown (fig 4), stitch a 1cm-long pear-shaped pearl drop bead to

50cm (20in) gold gauze wired ribbon
Pearl-covered jewellery mount
25 small pink-and-white fabric flowers
25 small yellow-and-white fabric flowers
Soft pink embroidery cotton
250 (approx) crystal rocailles
250 (approx) rainbow crystal drop beads

3 Make approx 16 long drops of alternating rainbow crystal drop beads and crystal rocailles. They should be long enough to hang below main tassel by 4–5cm (1¾–2in). Stitch drops to inside of tassel strands.
4 Make other shorter drops and stitch around base of tassel head.
5 Form a bow from gold gauze ribbon and stitch the pearl-covered mount, or a clump of tied pearls, to its centre. Stitch this to base of tassel head, with a crystal flower to either side of it.
6 Push pearl flower into top of tassel head above bow. Twist wire to secure.

16 4mm-diam rainbow faceted crystals
6 crystal rocailles
4 1cm-long pear-shaped pearl drop beads

base of tassel head of every alternate small tassel. Stitch 7 3mm-diam round pearls across top and base of tassel heads to finish.

fig 4

67

pin-beaded baubles

Here one basic shape is used to create three different designs. You could also adapt the idea to make Easter eggs or even a mobile for a child's room. All quantities of sequins given in the materials listed here are approximate.

Star bauble

You will need

Compressed cotton ball, 60mm
  (2½in) diameter
35gm approx gold-coloured lill pins
10gm approx silver-coloured lill pins
160 5mm-diam rainbow turquoise-blue
  cup sequins
160 5mm-diam rainbow pale blue
  cup sequins
70 5mm-diam silver cup sequins
40 tiny gold star sequins
30 silver pointed oval-shaped sequins
25 small silver star sequins
2 large turquoise rocailles
2 5mm-diam pale blue faceted beads

To make up

Use silver-coloured lill pins for all sequins except tiny gold stars, when gold-coloured pins should be used.

1 Mark ball into halves. At centre of line on one 'side', make a star using silver pointed oval-shaped sequins (fig 1).

2 Fill gap left in centre with a small silver star sequin. Pin in a tiny gold star sequin at each of the 5 angles of star, and 4 around central silver star sequin. Repeat at midpoint of opposite line, so that there is a 'front' and a 'back' star.

3 Outline stars with 5mm-diam rainbow turquoise-blue cup sequins, and then work 3 or 4 rounds of same sequins from this, pinning them unevenly on outer round and interspersing with 5mm-diam rainbow pale blue and 5mm-diam silver cup sequins. Complete the 'sky' with patches of 5mm-diam rainbow pale blue and silver cup sequins, and scatterings of tiny gold and small silver stars.

4 To finish, make a looped bow, using large turquoise rocailles and 5mm-diam pale blue faceted beads, to secure.

fig 1

Moon bauble

You will need

Compressed cotton ball, 6cm
(2½in) diameter
30cm (12in) approx dark blue satin
ribbon, 1cm (⅜in) wide
30gm approx gold-coloured lill pins
15gm approx silver-coloured lill pins
250 6mm-diam petrol-blue cup sequins
100 5mm-diam petrol-blue cup sequins
100 5mm-diam silver cup sequins
100 5mm-diam rainbow smoky
transparent cup sequins
40 5mm-diam rainbow transparent
cup sequins
20 small silver star sequins
2 large silver rocailles
2 5mm-diam petrol-blue faceted beads
Tracing paper

To make up

1 Mark out ball into quarters, like orange segments. If this is difficult to gauge freehand, slip an elastic band around ball to divide it in half, slip on another at right angles to this one, and then draw carefully alongside bands using a soft pencil.

2 Trace off moon pattern (fig 1) and cut out. Carefully pin tracing-paper moon at midpoint of one quarter line on ball, slanting it backwards slightly, and draw around it using a soft pencil (fig 2). Repeat this at midpoint of opposite

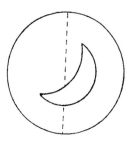

fig 1

quarter line, so that ball has a 'front' and a 'back' moon.

3 Using silver-coloured lill pins, pin bead moons by first pinning inside the shapes using 5mm-diam rainbow transparent cup sequins (fig 3).

4 Using silver-coloured lill pins and 5mm-diam silver cup sequins, fill in and outline moon shapes, pinning into drawn line for outline. Now draw a line between moons, looping to either side of other circle line (fig 4).

5 Using silver-coloured lill pins, pin along looping line using 5mm-diam rainbow smoky transparent cup sequins, adding a 5mm-diam silver cup sequin after every 3rd or 4th rainbow transparent cup sequin.

6 Using gold-coloured lill pins, pin 5mm-diam petrol-blue cup sequins around moons. Then fill in the 'sky', using a combination of 5mm- and 6mm-diam petrol-blue cup sequins – the different sequin sizes can reflect colour quite differently and will give added depth to the sky.

7 Using silver-coloured lill pins, pin a single small silver star sequins into the sky at random intervals, to give a scattered star effect.

8 To finish, cut ends of ribbon at a slant to prevent fraying and form the ribbon into a looped bow, securing each loop end with a dressmaking pin with the addition of a large silver rocaille, 5mm-diam petrol-blue faceted bead, and silver star sequin.

NB If using as a tree decoration, pin ribbon bow in at top of sky, at a slant to prevent pins pulling out when ball is suspended by the loop (see photograph page 62).

fig 2

fig 3

fig 4

Sun bauble

You will need

Compressed cotton ball, 60mm
  (2½in) diameter
25gm approx gold-coloured lill pins
20gm approx silver-coloured lill pins
360 3mm-diam gold flat sequins
300 5mm-diam brilliant sky-blue
  cup sequins

40 5mm-diam bronze cup sequins
25 5mm-diam rainbow cream-pink
  cup sequins
2 large iridescent bronze rocailles
2 5mm-diam bronze metallic
  faceted beads
Tracing paper

To make up

Use gold-coloured lill pins for pinning
the sun, and silver-coloured lill pins for
the 'sky'.

1 Mark ball into 2 halves using method
described for the moon bauble. Trace
off sun pattern (fig 1) and cut out.

2 Pin tracing-paper sun at midpoint of
line on one 'side' and draw around it
using a soft pencil. Repeat this at
midpoint of opposite line, so that ball
has a 'front' and a 'back' sun.

3 Pin a circle of 5mm-diam bronze cup
sequins into centre of sun. Pin 5mm-
diam rainbow cream-pink cup sequins
into left curve, and fill in rest of centre
with 5mm-diam bronze cup sequins
(fig 2).

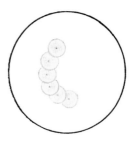

fig 2

4 Outline sun shape by pinning 3mm-
diam gold flat sequins into drawn line.
Fill in north, south, east and west sun
flares solidly with same sequins (fig 1).

5 Pin 5mm-diam rainbow cream-pink
cup sequins into central part of other 4
flares, and a 5mm-diam bronze cup
sequin at base of each; then complete
with 3mm-diam gold flat sequins.

6 Using 5mm-diam brilliant sky-blue cup
sequins, complete sky by filling between
the suns.

7 To finish, make a looped bow as for
the moon bauble, using large iridescent
bronze rocailles and 5mm-diam bronze
metallic faceted beads to secure.

Instead of finishing with a bow, try
decorating the bauble with the other
beading techniques you have mastered,
perhaps finishing with a tassel or a wire-
beaded flower, for example. You could
also experiment making several balls
with the same motif but in different
sizes. Alternative bauble designs can be
found on page 106.

fig 1

71

wire-beaded flowers

Wire-beading was particularly popular in Venice in the eighteenth century when gondolas, altars and domestic interiors were traditionally decorated with wire-beaded flowers. Here basic flower and leaf designs are used for a variety of decorative items – to form the basis of a pretty posy which would look lovely as a dining table centrepiece or resting on a mantelpiece, to grace a highly original hatpin and to embellish a brooch to make a fetching floral corsage.

Forget-me-not posy

You will need

Reel wire and green silk floss
Reel thicker wire 20cm (8in) long approx
300 approx of following rocailles:
Dark green transparent (dk gr trs roc)
Lime-green transparent (lim-gr trs roc)
Red transparent (rd trs roc)
Pink-lined transparent (pk-lnd trs roc)
Blue-lined transparent (bl-lnd trs roc)

Pale turquoise (ple turq roc)
Yellow (yel roc)
Pearl (prl roc)
200 approx of following 2mm cut bugles:
Pale blue (2m ple bl cut bg)
Red (2m rd cut bg)
Dark green (2m dk gr cut bg)
Pearly-white (2m prl-wh cut bg)

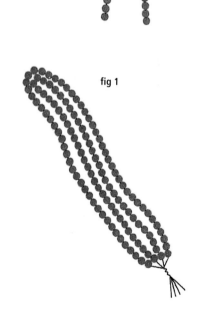

fig 1

To make up

1 Using 6 2m dk gr cut bg per branch, make 1 14-branch and 2 12-branch leaf sprays, following step 6 of the hatpin instructions overleaf.

2 Using 7 dk gr trs roc per branch, make 3 7-branch and 3 8-branch leaf sprays, as described overleaf.

3 Using 7 lim-gr trs roc per branch, make 1 7-branch, 1 8-branch, and 2 11-branch leaf sprays, as described overleaf.

4 Make 2 loops of 90 lim-gr trs roc, twist together at their centres and pinch together to make long tulip-like leaves (fig 1).

5 Repeat step 4 twice more, then make 3 more leaves using dk gr trs roc.

6 Following figs 1–5 on page 63, make 9 forget-me-not flowers using ple turq roc and 1 yel roc for each centre.

7 Make 12 similar flowers using pk-lnd trs roc, 6 using bl-lnd trs roc, and 3 using rd trs roc. Make 2 similar but 4-

petalled flowers, using 2m ple bl cut bg.

8 Following step 2 of the corsage instructions on page 75, make 5 3-leaf sprays using dk gr trs roc, and 3 3-leaf sprays using lim-gr trs roc.

9 Using dk gr trs roc make a fern-type leaf following steps shown in fig 2.

10 Make 14 more fern-type leaves using dk gr trs roc, and 12 similar leaves using lim-gr trs roc. Twist together 3 of the same colour, to make a 3-branch spray.

11 Form a red rose petal by making rounds of 11, 15, 19, 23, 27 and 31 rd trs roc, working from inside loop outwards. Repeat 3 times to make a total of 4 petals. Work 3 smaller petals for centre, and 5 single loops of 9 beads each for stamens.
Repeat once more, and make 1 similar using 2m rd cut bg.

12 Make 3 3-petal flowers, using rounds of 20, 25 and 30 prl roc per petal, and 3 stamens, each of a loop of 12 yel roc.

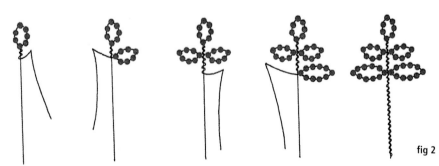

fig 2

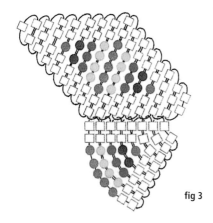

fig 3

13 To make butterflies, work top wings following fig 3 and using the same technique as for flower petals on page 66. Work bottom wings by following fig 3, but this time intertwine each row with top wing .

14 Make butterfly body following fig 4.

15 To complete butterfly, slip wire ends of wings into side wires of body, thread back inside beads and cut off neatly.

16 Take each finished piece of posy and twist it to a length of thicker wire for the stem, then cover with green silk

floss as shown in figs 6–7 on page 63. Finish bouquet as described on page 63.

17 Position butterflies as though they had just flown to rest on the posy.

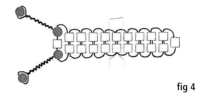

fig 4

Hatpin

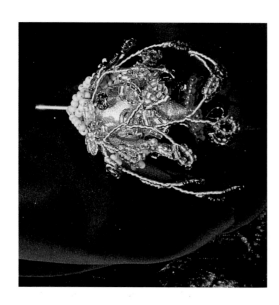

You will need

Hatpin stalk with point protector
Pear-shaped compressed cotton shape
15m (16yd) approx wire and green
  silk floss
Bodkin or stiletto
Gold craft paint or spray
Craft glue
80 approx of following rocailles:

To make up

1 Make a 3mm (⅛in) diameter hole in rounded end of pear shape, by pushing in a bodkin or stiletto about 1.5cm (⅝in) deep. Paint or spray pear shape using gold craft paint and leave to dry.

2 Make 3 5-petalled forget-me-nots, by threading on 9 ple turq roc and twisting to make 1 petal (figs 1–5 on page 63).

3 Make 1 similar flower, using 9 pk-lnd cut bg per petal, and 1 yel roc for stamen. Make 2 more flowers, with only 4 petals, using ple bl-lnd cut bg, 9 per petal, and 1 pk-lnd cut bg for stamen.

4 Make 1 similar 5-petalled flower, using 13 red transparent rocailles per

Dark green transparent (dk gr trs roc)
Lime-green transparent (lim-gr trs roc)
Red transparent (rd trs roc)
Pale turquoise (ple turq roc)
Yellow (yel roc)
50 2mm pale blue-lined cut bugles
  (ple bl-lnd cut bg)
50 2mm pink-lined cut bugles
  (pk-lnd cut bg)

petal. Twist wire stem tight and cut to 2cm (¾in), coat this with craft glue and push down into top of pear shape.

5 Twist stems of the 1 pink and 2 pale blue flowers tight and cut to 5mm (¼in). Coat with craft glue and push into pear shape half-way down, spacing flowers around circumference.

6 Using 7 dk gr trs roc per branch, make a 5-branched spray as shown in fig 1.

7 Make another spray of dk gr trs roc, 2 sprays of lim-gr trs roc , and 1 spray with branches 1, 4 and 5 of dark green, and branches 2 and 3 of lim-gr trs roc.

8 Cover spray stems with green silk floss (see figs 6–7, page 63).

9 Put craft glue into hole in base of pear shape and insert sprays, spacing them around circumference of pear. Cover 2cm (¾in) of 2 of forget-me-not stems with green silk floss and insert these into hole. Now insert hatpin stalk into centre of wires and hole, and push a forget-me-not next to it, so that petals of flower nestle around stalk and hatpin appears to be coming out of centre.

10 Bend sprays over pear shape.

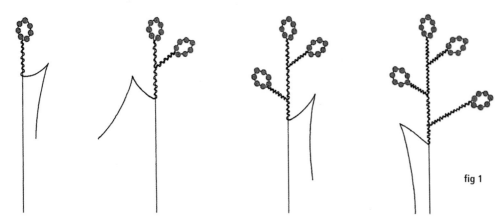

fig 1

Corsage

You will need

Large brooch or tie pin
Dark green metal claw-mounted
 embroidery stone
Reel wire and green silk floss
100 approx of following rocailles:
Dark green transparent (dk gr trs roc)
Lime-green transparent (lim-gr trs roc)
Red transparent (rd trs roc)

Pink-lined transparent (pk-lnd trs roc)
Pale turquoise (ple turq roc)
Yellow (yel roc)
White (wh roc)
Gold metallic (gld met roc)
Pearl (prl roc)
60 2mm pale blue cut bugles
 (ple bl cut bg)

To make up

1 Make 6 individual leaves, using rounds of 8, 18 and 28 dk gr trs roc, pinch at top to make a leaf shape (fig 1).

fig 1

2 Make 1 3-leaf spray using same leaf (fig 2).

3 Make 3 5-petalled forget-me-nots (see technique on page 63). Make 2 similar flowers using pk-lnd trs roc, each with 1 yel roc and 1 ple turq roc for stamen.

4 Using same number of beads per round as for dark green leaves, make 1 4-petalled flower using rd trs roc, leaving wire rounded. Make 1 flower as forget-me-not using gld met roc with a

prl roc picot centre. Twist this with red flower, to make gold flower its centre.

5 Repeat instructions making 1 4-petalled flower of ple bl cut bg with a 'forget-me-not' centre of gld met roc.

6 Form a flower from 9 loops of rd trs roc and 9 loops of wh roc (fig 3). Continue twisting together.

7 Following fig 1 of the hatpin shown opposite, make 2 5-branched leaf sprays of 7 dk gr trs roc each, 1 spray of lim-gr trs roc, and 1 spray of mixed gr trs roc.

8 Make 3 loops of 7 rd trs roc, following fig 3, and repeat once.

9 Cover all stems with green silk floss, (see figs 6–7 on page 63). Lay leaf sprays and flowers together, as if arranging a tiny bouquet, varying the lengths. Twist all together and, leaving approx 1.5cm (⅝in) of wrapped stems protruding over one end of the pin, bind to the brooch or tie pin with wire, then wrap green silk floss over this.

10 To finish, attach the embroidery stone to centre of 1 dark green leaf, carefully bend out flower petals and arrange the sprays as required.

fig 2

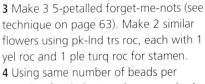

fig 3

75

Bead embellishments

Beads can add richness and texture when used to embellish the surface of a fabric, either as an abstract adornment or to represent and to emphasize a feature of a figurative form, such as the canvaswork blue poppy cushion and the beaded strawberry and pear designs seen in this chapter. Beads can be also be incorporated to beautiful effect with other textile crafts where they form an integral part of the technique. A good example of this is the original cloche and mittens design, where knitting and beading combine with dramatic results.

surface beading

Beads and sequins are a highly versatile method of embellishment. You can use them to decorative effect on many furnishing fabrics – from felt and chintz to velvet and silk. Adding beads as an ornamental touch to a ready-stitched canvaswork design can also be attractive. Further, they can be combined with many other craft techniques, such as crochet or bobbin lace. Here are just a few ideas, but you could try experimenting with any of your favourite textile techniques.

Bead embroidery

There are two methods of using beads or sequins as an embellishment to the surface of a fabric. They can either be combined with other thread embroidery techniques or simply stitched on. This idea has already been explored in miniature with the beaded buttons on pages 44–47; in this chapter it has been employed to decorate three-dimensional 'beaded fruits', representing and emphasizing the fruits' features.

These themes can be developed further by applying beads to a textured ground fabric, such as a damask or tapestry weave, with the beads used to enhance the fabric design. With a plain fabric the embroidered beads may form the dominant feature, but when they are incorporated with a textured fabric usually each will enhance the inherent qualities of the other. To design and work both the ground fabric and the beading can present exciting and challenging possibilities, as shown in the cushion on page 82, where the poppy characteristics are perfect for embellishing with beading.

Beading on finished canvaswork

When using beads or sequins to decorate ready-stitched canvaswork designs, such as the cushion on page 82, it is best to pick colours that will contrast with the stitching. When choosing the size of the beads, take into consideration the end use: on a cushion, for instance, it might prove better to use small beads which will nestle into the wool of the canvaswork, bugles which will follow the direction of the stitched background, or even Japanese magatamas, rather than large beads which could prove a little uncomfortable.

1 Use tent stitch to cover the background (fig 1). When starting off, leave a long loose end of yarn at back of canvas and work first few stitches from right to left over it. Work following row of stitches below last row. Continue working alternately from right to left, then from left to right (fig 2).
2 When starting a new thread next to an area that has already been stitched, simply run thread through the back of a few stitches to secure and then bring needle out to front of canvaswork at position required.
3 To attach a bead when canvaswork is completed, use strong sewing thread to match bead and a needle fine enough to pass through bead hole. Fasten on by using a large knot or making one or two fastening-on stitches on back of canvas. Stitch into place.
4 Fasten off neatly on back of canvas.

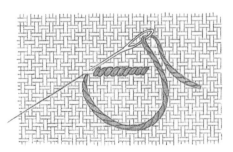

fig 1

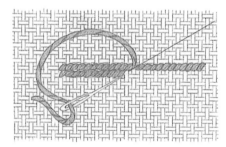

fig 2

Beading on fabric

To create the decorative effect used in the beaded pear and strawberry seen on pages 85–87, choose sequins and beads to complement the fabric and to represent naturalistically the features of the fruits.

You could also use this technique to add extra texture to soft furnishing accessories such as cushions and bolsters, for example.

1 Cut a length of sewing thread and pull it several times through a small block of beeswax for ease of working.

2 Make a large knot, bring needle through fabric to the point where you wish to position a sequin, and thread on a sequin.

3 Thread on a bead of your choice, then pass needle back down through sequin hole so that bead is anchoring sequin to fabric. Make a few fastening-off stitches on reverse side of fabric and cut off thread neatly.

4 Repeat this sequence with all sequins until you have achieved your desired decorative effect. You can experiment by varying the colour combination of beads and sequins.

For more ideas for combining beading with other embroidery techniques, see the information on couching overleaf. Beading can also be combined with applique, as with the denim shirt design on page 94.

Bead knitting

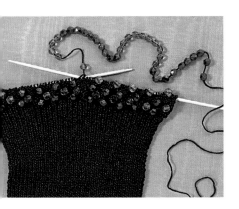

Beads can add an extra dimension to knitting. You can bead a motif, integrating beads into the knitting pattern, as with the cloche and mittens on page 88-93. You can also add beads as a finishing touch, as with the picot edging in the same pattern. Always consider the end use of the knitted item, being careful not to add beads where it would be impractical.

If incorporating beads into a knitting pattern, careful charting of your design is essential, so that you can accurately thread your chosen beads on to your working yarn. If you are knitting a large area or using heavy beads, be prepared to thread only as many beads as you need for the first one or two rows in order to minimize the possibility of breaking the yarn.

In bead knitting, the best way of guaranteeing success is always to slip a stitch (fig 1) before pushing up a bead to the work (fig 2). This ensures that the bead will lie neatly across the front of the knitting and does not slip through to the reverse side of the finished article.

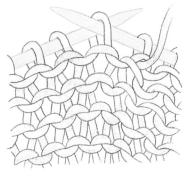

fig 1

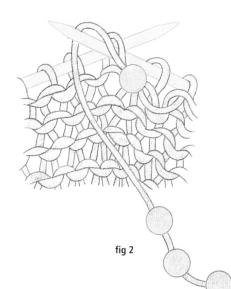

fig 2

Other surface beading

In the same way that beads can be incorporated with knitting, they can be also be integrated into other craft techniques. The pattern on pages 88–93 could be adapted to crochet, for example. With bead crochet, as with bead knitting, charting and threading are the most important criteria. You could either thread the beads on to the crochet cotton or yarn and pass them gently up the working yarn when required, or, if the bead hole diameter is large enough to accommodate the crochet hook, hook the beads individually when they are required.

Beads can also be incorporated while working on canvas, as a beaded motif with a tent stitch background, for instance, in which case the beads are stitched to the canvas first, using doubled sewing cotton or single polyester thread and the background is worked once the beads are in place. Alternatively, beads and thread can be used for each tent stitch, resulting in a totally beaded canvas. It is important to consider the use of the finished canvaswork when deciding which method to apply.

Beads and bobbin lace are another effective combination. Here the beads are threaded first, usually on to the same yarn as that used for the lace, and wound on to a separate bobbin. This is then worked into the lace pattern using only the yarn until a bead is required, when the bead is pushed up to the right position, the bobbins twisted and the bead bobbin used for the yarn only until the next bead required.

Couched beading

An interesting way to use surface beading is to decorate a printed or woven motif with beads, and then appliqué the beaded motif to another fabric. This is the technique used for the project on pages 94–96, in which a printed blue-and-white plate and fruit dish motif has been beaded and then applied to a blue denim shirt, to striking effect.

The method used to attach the beads to the motif is called 'couching'. Couching is used for certain beaded designs, as it produces a smoother profile and better linear effect than stitching down each bead individually through its hole. By pushing the beads close together on the thread being couched, you will be able to achieve a more continuous line than when stitching them individually.

Couching is an embroidery technique often used to apply a thread or yarn which is too thick to be stitched into the fabric ground; instead, it is held to the fabric by 'couching' it down with a finer thread. Bead couching is worked as follows.

1 Lay down a pre-strung length of beads to follow design line.
2 Stitch over this thread using a separate, finer thread, working stitches over thread between beads (figs 1–3).

3 After couching down each bead, slide next one up close to it, and couch down thread between that bead and the next.

fig 1   fig 2   fig 3

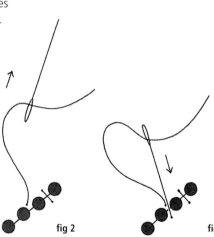

Couched leaf This leaf design is a simple motif that would look striking stitched as a repeat motif on a plain fabric such as damask, although any firm woven fabric would be suitable. You could use it to make a tablecloth, for example, complemented by matching napkins. Alternatively, you could use it on an item of clothing, such as a waistcoat or a pocket.

1 Draw leaf design on to fabric and then mount in an embroidery hoop or frame – it is difficult to avoid puckering if couching unstretched fabric.

2 Thread 40cm (16in) approx polyester thread, make a fastening-on stitch and bring needle through to front of fabric at B in fig 1. Thread on 25 dark green rocailles (dk gr roc).

3 Thread another needle with 50cm (20in) approx sewing thread, make a fastening-on stitch, then bring needle through to front of fabric, one bead length up centre leaf vein line from B.

4 Pulling bead thread taut, stitch ('couch') down over it with sewing thread, then advance needle below fabric one more bead length up centre leaf vein line.

5 Repeat step 4, following drawn line carefully and pulling bead thread taut each time, as far as A. Thread both needles one after the other through stitches on reverse of fabric as far as C.

6 Bring bead thread needle through to front of fabric at right-hand side of centre leaf vein line, and thread approx 50 leaf-green rocailles (lf-gr roc).

7 Bring sewing thread needle to front of fabric one bead length down outside leaf line. Working as before, couch down this line as far as D. Thread both needles one after the other through stitches on reverse of fabric as far as B.

8 Working as before, couch up outside leaf line as far as C, adding more lf-gr roc to bead thread if necessary, or slipping off any excess.

9 Bring bead thread needle through to front of fabric, one half bead width below outside leaf line on right of centre leaf vein line and close to it. Then bring sewing thread needle through to front of fabric, one bead length below bead thread.

10 Next work 13 short filling-in rows from C to B down right-hand side of leaf. Thread 5 dk gr roc and 1 lf-gr roc on to bead thread, then couch down with sewing thread following curve of outside leaf line.

11 Bring both needles through to front of fabric at E. Thread 6 lf-gr roc on to bead thread and couch up to centre leaf vein line again, following curve of last line couched.

12 Continue down leaf in this way, threading and couching down each row as follows: 5 dk gr roc and 1 lf-gr roc; 7 lf-gr roc; 5 dk gr roc and 1 lf-gr roc; 7 lf-gr roc; 4 dk gr roc and 2 lf-gr roc; 6 lf-gr roc; 3 dk gr roc and 3 lf-gr roc; 5 lf-gr roc; 3 dk gr roc and 2 lf-gr roc; 4 lf gr roc; 1 dk gr roc and 3 lf-gr roc.

13 Bring both needles through to front of fabric just above B. Working towards and away from centre leaf vein line alternately, and filling in upwards towards C, thread and couch down each row as follows: 3 lf-gr roc; 2 dk gr roc; 5 lf gr roc; 7 dk gr roc and 1 leaf-gr roc; 8 lf-gr roc; 7 dk gr roc and 1 lf-gr roc; 9 lf-gr roc; 8 dk gr roc and 1 lf-gr roc. Make 1 or 2 fastening-off stitches on reverse side of fabric and cut off threads neatly.

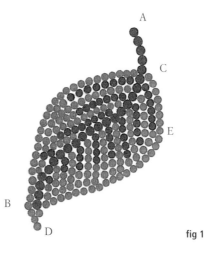

fig 1

blue poppy cushion

This design involves an effective combination of stitching and beading. Essentially, the background is stitched first and the beads added as an embellishment, accentuating the characteristics of the poppy flower. Some of the beads used here are Japanese in origin. Known as magatama beads, they have an off-centre hole and will therefore hang at any angle allowing them to lie along the stitching.

Alternative finishes to the cushion might be the addition of a ready-made upholstery fringe or piping with a satin-biased edging, picking up on the colour of the beads. Looped beaded tassels, finished with a bead drop in the corners might be attractive, too. All bead quantities given in this design are approximate.

You will need

30.5cm (12in) square double-thread ecru canvas, 10 holes to 2.5cm (1in)
Paterna tapestry wool in colours shown on chart overleaf
Tapestry needle size 18 or 20
Sewing thread to match bead colours
Sewing needle
Small rectangular tapestry frame (optional)

59 3mm-diam green metallic beads
50 4mm-diam yellow glass beads
32 9mm-long lilac-purple bugles
25 lilac-purple magatamas
22 3mm-diam turquoise-blue metallic beads
17 4mm-diam cerise wooden beads
17 9mm-long pale turquoise bugles
15 large lilac-blue rocailles

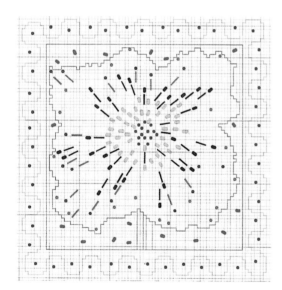

fig 1

To make up

The finished needlepoint measures 21 cm (8½in) square.

1 Fold canvas both horizontally and vertically, and sew a running stitch along both folds to find centre point.
2 The needlepoint is worked using tent stitch (see page 78) and 2 strands of tapestry wool throughout. Each working length of wool should be no more than 40cm (16in). Start at centre point and work outwards, finishing with the background last.
3 Using sewing thread and needle, stitch beads over surface of needlepoint following chart (fig 1). Sew bugles to radiate outwards from centre of poppy, following direction of petal veins. If not sewing each bead individually, it is best to make a fastening-off stitch before advancing on reverse side to next beading point.
NB If you have not used a frame to work the needlepoint, it may be necessary to stretch the finished work, following the instructions given here. It is essential to do this just before making up the cushion, as it will go out of shape again in about a day.

To stretch the finished work

1 Using a clean board, larger than the piece of work, lay down a sheet of plastic or polythene, and a piece of cotton, such as sheeting. Be careful to check that the board is square: i.e. has 4 right-angled corners.
2 Spray needlepoint lightly with water, or dampen with a moist sponge. Place the top edge of the canvas parallel with the top edge of the board, rightside facing upwards.
3 Using tacks or nails, beginning in the centre of the top edge of the unworked canvas, pin out first to the lefthand side, and then to the righthand side, with the pins inserted at regular intervals of approx. 2cm (¾in).
4 Pin the bottom edge of the unworked canvas in the same way, using a set square to check that the sides are at right angles to the top top and bottom edges. Then pin lefthand side edge, and then righthand side.
5 Lay board flat and allow the work to dry naturally. This may be several days. If the work is very distorted, it might be necessary to repeat the process to obtain a really good finish.

520   353   302   543   553   554   620   632   771   772

beaded fruits

Beads and sequins are used here to add sparkle and extra definition to these fabric fruits. This technique works best on firm-woven fabrics, such as velvet, damask or cotton chintz. To give added depth and richness of colour, try using layers of different coloured organza, echoing the bloom on the fruits themselves. Other fruits would also make attractive shapes for beading.

Strawberry

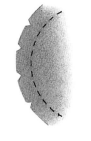

fig 1

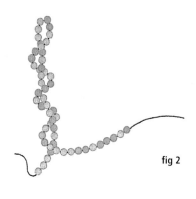

fig 2

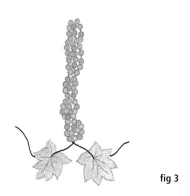

fig 3

You will need

30 x 15cm (12 x 6in) red velvet
50cm (20in) silver-coloured jewellery
    wire
Small pack polyester wadding
Small block beeswax
Tracing paper
Pattern-cutting carbon
Sewing thread to match fabric
Beading or fine straw needle
120 2mm gold bugles
120 5mm-diam transparent iridescent
    pale gold cup sequins
100 apple-green rocailles
50 jade-green rocailles
5 pale green leaf-shaped beads

To make up

1 Trace strawberry pattern on page 109 and cut out.
2 Pin pattern to wrong side of velvet, with a layer of carbon between pattern and fabric, taking care to follow grain line instruction. Mark opening and 'pips', and cut out. Repeat twice more, to make 3 identical pattern pieces.
3 To sequin the strawberry, use pale gold cup sequins, cup uppermost, and gold cut bugles and follow method described on page 79.
4 Pin fabric shapes wrong sides together and tack seams, leaving a 3cm (1¼in) opening at top edge for stuffing and to attach stem. Machine stitch, then clip seams at 2cm (¾in) intervals (fig 1).
5 Using a zigzag machine stitch, oversew seams to prevent velvet fraying, then turn right side out.

6 Stuff really tightly with polyester wadding. You might find it helpful to use the end of a pencil to push wadding into curves of strawberry if necessary. Turn in remaining seams and hand stitch them together, leaving a 1cm (⅜in) opening for stem.
7 For the stem, cut a 50cm (20in) length of silver-coloured jewellery wire and fold over one end by about 2cm (¾in) to prevent beads slipping off. Begin threading wire with a random mix of apple-green and jade-green rocailles. When you have threaded about 10cm (4in), bend wire over, thread another 10cm (4in) and twist this length around 1st 10cm (4in). Repeat this sequence, moving up and then down stem (fig 2). It is not necessary to cover all wire with beads for last 2 twists; some wire showing through will give stems a more delicate look.
8 Make sure there is an unbeaded length of wire left at end, and unbend 2cm (¾in) first turned over. On to each of these 2 ends, thread a pale green leaf-shaped bead (fig 3), and secure by twisting ends together (fig 4).
9 Push completed stem into hole left in top of strawberry, then finish sewing seams together, passing thread through twisted wire a few times to secure stem.
10 Complete strawberry by sewing the other 3 green leaf shapes around base of stem below 1st 2 leaf-shape beads.

fig 4

85

Pear

You will need

35 x 15cm (14 x 6in) lime-green glazed
  cotton chintz
30cm (12in) silver-coloured jewellery
  wire
Small pack polyester wadding
Small block beeswax
Tracing paper
Pattern-cutting carbon
Sewing thread to match fabric
Beading or fine straw needle
180 lime-green rocailles
180 5mm-diam transparent iridescent
  pale gold cup sequins
20 green rocailles
1 brown rocaille
1 8mm-diam copper cup sequin

To make up

1 Trace pear pattern and 3 speckle mark
guides on page 109, and cut out
carefully on fabric.

2 Pin pattern to wrong side of chintz,
with a layer of carbon between pattern
and fabric, being careful to follow grain
line instruction. Mark opening and
speckles, and cut out. Repeat twice
more, to make 3 identical pattern
pieces. Next, again using carbon, trace
speckle marks from 3 pattern pieces to
3 fabric pieces.

3 To sequin the pear, use pale gold
sequins and lime-green rocailles and
follow method described on page 79.

4 Pin fabric shapes wrong sides together
and tack seams, leaving a 1cm (⅜in)
opening at top for inserting stem, and a
4cm (1½in) opening at bottom for
stuffing (see pattern). Machine stitch,
then clip seams at 2cm (¾in) intervals as
for strawberry.

5 Turn right side out. Stuff with
polyester wadding until a firm, really
tightly stuffed pear shape has been
formed. Use the end of a pencil to push
wadding into curves of pear if
necessary. Carefully turn in bottom
seams and hand stitch them together.

6 For the stem, cut a 30cm (12in) length
of silver-coloured jewellery wire and fold
over one end by about 2cm (¾in) to

prevent beads slipping off. Begin
threading wire with a random mix of
lime-green and green rocailles. When
you have threaded about 5cm (2in),
bend wire over, thread another 5cm
(2in) and twist this length around first
5cm (2in). Repeat this sequence, moving
up and then down stem as for
strawberry on previous page.

fig 1

7 Make sure there is an unbeaded length of wire at end, twist this around initial loop and then push completed stem into hole left in top of pear. Finish sewing seams together, passing thread through twisted wire a few times to secure stem, and finish by bending into a realistic pear stem.

8 Complete by stitching the copper cup sequin convex side outermost, anchored by the brown rocaille (fig 1).

Alternative finishes might involve using a fabric dye pen to create blemishes and bruises. You could also reduce the pattern pieces to make a branch of different sized pears, to be attached to a main stem, made using the method for the individual stalks.

cloche & mittens

This beaded cloche and mittens ensemble, the chief feature of which is a beautiful beaded triangle, evokes another age, when dressing to dine and dance was de rigueur. Knitting needles, yarn and beautiful faceted crystal beads combine to capture the glamour of the 1920s. The charts accompanying the pattern indicate the bead threading sequence only, not the number of stitches and rows.

Used in combination with different yarns, cotton or silk perhaps, and appropriate beads, the beaded triangle could be repeated as an original edging for a blind, shelf or a footstool, or used individually as a decorative feature to be applied to the neckline, shoulders or the waist of garments.

Cloche

Tension

28 sts to 5cm (2in) over single rib unstretched, using 2¾mm (US size 2) knitting needles

Abbreviations

bd	bead
K	knit
lg	large
P	purl
pu	push up
psso	pass slipped st over
rem	remain(s)(ing)
rep	repeat
rnd(s)	round(s)
RS	right side
sl	slip purlwise
sm	small
st(s)	stitch(es)
sm	small
tog	together
WS	wrong side
yrn	yarn round needle

You will need

Pair of 2¾mm (US size 2) knitting
  needles for cloche rib and mittens
Set 2¾mm (US size 2) double-pointed
  knitting needles for cloche crown
150 gm (6 oz) ball 3-ply metallic
  knitting yarn
2 stitch holders
Large-eyed needle which will pass
  smoothly through all beads
For threading to knit cloche and mittens:
  435 small petrol-blue beads
  147 large purple faceted beads
  22 large pink faceted crystals
For triangles and mitten picots:
  414 small petrol-blue beads
For cloche crown:
  1 large purple faceted bead

To make

Using 2¾mm (US size 2) needles, cast on 194 sts and work single (K1, P1) rib for 13cm (5in).
Next row (RS) Slip 1 knitwise, K1, psso, K to last 2 sts, K2 tog. 192 sts rem. The first and last decreased sts of last row will form the rib seam.
Next row (WS) *K2 tog; repeat from *. 96 sts rem.
Cut off yarn. Transfer the rem 96 sts to three of the set of four double-pointed needles (31 sts on each needle).
Sew rib seam tog.
Set aside rib until it is needed again.

To thread beads for crown

Using large-eyed needle, thread beads on to ball of yarn, following bead sequence chart opposite (fig 1).

Beginning at point A, read from right to left to point B and thread on a large purple faceted bead, a small petrol-blue bead, a large purple faceted bead and so on as indicated.

Move up to point B above this, and reading now from left to right to point C, thread on 7 large purple faceted beads as indicated.

Continue reading from the chart and threading on beads in this way until you reach point U, smoothing beads gently

For cloche triangle tassel:
  3 small petrol-blue beads
  2 large black rocailles
  2 small greeny blue beads
  1 large purple faceted bead
  1 large pink faceted crystal
  1 purple drop bead
For tassel strands:
  264 black cut rocailles
  96 greeny blue cut rocailles
  64 4mm amethyst bugles
  8 pink crystal rocailles
  8 8mm amethyst bugles
  8 6mm amethyst bugles
For mitten loops:
  78 garnet rocailles
  2 small petrol-blue beads
  2 large purple faceted beads

down yarn as you progress, so that you have about 30cm (12in) of yarn beyond the threaded beads at point U.

To make the crown

Using the end of the yarn beyond the threaded beads and gently sliding beads up as required, work the pattern in the round with RS (purl side) always facing as follows:
1st rnd (RS) P2, *sl 1, pu lg bd, P3, sl 1, pu sm bd, P3; rep from * 11 times more, ending last rep P1.
2nd, 4th, 6th and 8th rnds Purl.
3rd rnd Using sm bds only, P2, *sl 1, pu bd, P3; rep from *.
5th rnd P2, *sl 1, pu sm bd, P3, sl 1, pu lg bd; rep from * 11 times more, ending last rep P1.
7th rnd As 3rd rnd.
9th rnd As first rnd.
10th rnd *P3, P2 tog, P6, P2 tog; rep from * to last 5 sts, ending P3, P2 tog. 81 sts.
11th, 13th, 15th, 17th, 21st, 23rd and 25th rnds Purl.
12th rnd *P2 tog, yrn; rep from * to last st, P1.
14th rnd As 12th rnd.
16th rnd P2 tog, *P2 tog, P3; rep from *, ending last rep P2. 64 sts.
18th rnd *P3, sl 1, pu lg bd, P3, sl 1, pu

sm bd; rep from * 7 times more.

20th rnd Using sm bds only, P1, *sl 1, pu sm bd, P3; rep from *, ending last rep P2.

22nd rnd *P3, sl 1, pu sm bd, P3, sl 1, pu lg bd; rep from * 7 times more.

24th rnd As 20th rnd.

26th rnd As 18th rnd.

27th rnd *P6, P2 tog; rep from * 7 times more. 56 sts.

28th rnd *P2 tog, yrn; rep from *.

29th rnd Purl.

30th rnd As 28th rnd.

31st rnd *P5, P2 tog; rep from *. 48 sts.

32nd rnd Purl.

33rd, 35th, 37th and 39th rnds Purl.

34th rnd *P3, sl 1, pu sm bd, P3, sl 1, pu lg bd; rep from * 5 times more.

36th rnd Using sm bds only, *P1, sl 1, pu bd; rep from * to last 2 sts, P2.

38th rnd *P3, sl 1, pu lg bd, P3, sl 1, pu sm bd; rep from * 5 times more.

40th rnd As 36th rnd.

41st rnd *P2, P2 tog; rep from *. 36 sts.

42nd rnd *P2, sl 1, pu lg bd, P2, sl 1, pu sm bd; rep from * 5 times more.

43rd rnd *P5, P2 tog; rep from * 5 times

more. 30 sts.

44th rnd Using sm bds only, *sl 1, pu bd, P2; rep from * 9 times more.

45th rnd *P3, P2 tog; rep from * 5 times more. 24 sts.

46th rnd *P1, sl 1, pu lg bd, P1, sl 1, pu sm bd; rep from * 5 times more.

47th rnd *P2, P2 tog; rep from * 5 times more. 18 sts.

48th rnd *Sl 1, pu lg bd, P1; rep from * 8 times more.

49th rnd *P2, P2 tog; rep from * 3 times more, P2. 14 sts.

50th rnd *Sl 1, pu lg bd, P1; rep from * 6 times more.

51st rnd P3, (P2 tog, P1) twice, P2 tog. P3. 11 sts.

52nd rnd *Sl 1, pu sm bd, P1, sl 1, pu lg bd, P1; rep from * twice more, omitting P1 at end of last rep.

53rd rnd (P2 tog) 5 times, P1. 6 sts. Cut off yarn, leaving an end about 20cm (8in) long. Thread end through rem 6 sts. Pull the yarn tight and secure with a few stitches. Slip a large purple bead on to the yarn, sew it at the apex of the crown and finish off neatly.

fig 1

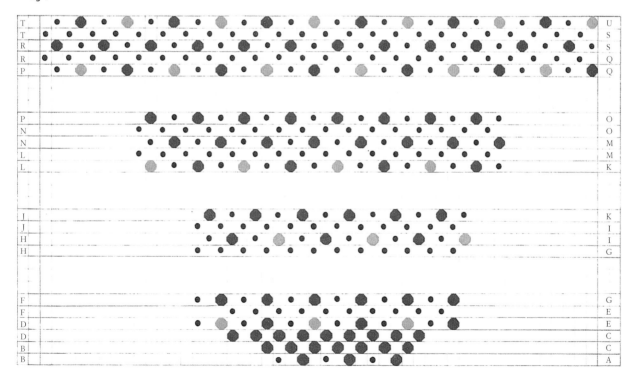

To thread beads for cloche triangle

The beaded triangle is made separately and sewn on to the cloche. Before casting on the sts, the beads should be threaded on to the yarn.

**Using large-eyed needle, thread beads on to ball of yarn, following bead sequence chart below (fig 2).

Beginning at point A, read from right to left to point B and thread on a small petrol-blue bead as indicated.

Move up to point B above this and, reading now from left to right to reach point C, thread on two small petrol-blue beads as indicated.

Move up to point C above this and, reading now from right to left to point D, thread on one small petrol-blue bead, one large pink faceted crystal and one small petrol-blue bead as indicated.

Continue reading from chart and threading beads on to ball of yarn in this way until you reach point O, smoothing the beads gently down yarn as you progress so that you have about 30cm (12in) of yarn beyond the threaded beads at point O.**

To make the beaded triangle for cloche

Using 2¾mm (US size 2) needles and the end of the yarn beyond the threaded beads, cast on 29 sts for the cloche triangle.

***Gently sliding beads up as required, work the pattern back and forth in rows as follows:

1st row K2, sl 1, pu sm bd, *K1, sl 1, pu sm bd, K1, sl 1, pu lg bd; rep from * 4 times more, (K1, sl 1, pu sm bd) twice, K2.

2nd row Knit.

3rd row K1, *K2 tog, yf; rep from * to last 2 sts, K2.

4th and 5th rows Repeat last 2 rows once more.

6th row Knit.

7th row K2, *sl 1, pu sm bd, K1, sl 1, pu lg bd, K1; rep from * 5 times more, sl 1, pu sm bd, K2.

8th row K2 tog, K1, *sl 1, pu sm bd, K1; rep from * 10 times more, sl 1, pu sm bd, K1, K2 tog.

9th row K2 tog, K1, *sl 1, pu sm bd, K1, sl 1, pu lg bd, K1; rep from * 4 times more, sl 1, pu sm bd, K1, K2 tog.

10th row K2 tog, K1, *sl 1, pu sm bd, K1; rep from * 8 times more, sl 1, pu sm bd, K1, K2 tog.

11th row K2 tog, K1, *sl 1, pu sm bd, K1, sl 1, pu lg bd, K1; rep from * 3 times more, sl 1, pu sm bd, K1, K2 tog.

12th row K2 tog, K1, *sl 1, pu sm bd, K1; rep from * 6 times more, sl 1, pu sm bd, K1, K2 tog.

13th row K2 tog, K1, *sl 1, pu sm bd, K1, sl 1, pu lg bd, K1; rep from * 2 times more, sl 1, pu sm bd, K1, K2 tog.

14th row K2 tog, K1, *sl 1, pu sm bd, K1; rep from * 4 times more, sl 1, pu sm bd , K1, K2 tog.

15th row K2 tog, K1, *sl 1, pu sm bd, K1, sl 1, pu lg bd, K1; rep from * once more, sl 1, pu sm bd, K1, K2 tog.

16th row K2 tog, K1, *sl 1, pu sm bd, K1; rep from * 2 times more, sl 1, pu sm bd, K1, K2 tog.

17th row K2 tog, K1, sl 1, pu sm bd, K1, sl 1, pu lg bd, K1, sl 1, pu sm bd, K1, K2 tog.

fig 2

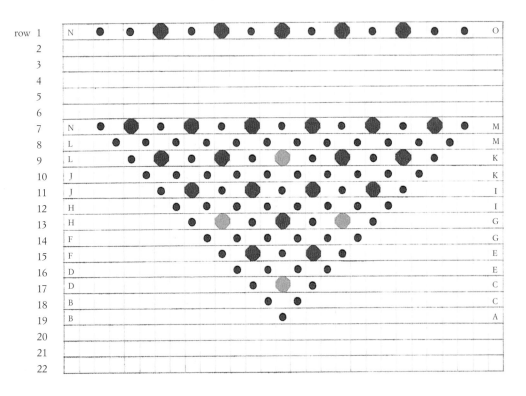

18th row K2 tog, K1, sl 1, pu sm bd, K1, sl 1, pu sm bd, K1, K2 tog.

19th row K2 tog, K1, sl 1, pu sm bd, K1, K2 tog.

20th row Knit.

21st row K2 tog, K1, K2 tog.

22nd row K3 tog.

Cut off yarn, leaving an end about 10cm (4in) long.

To fasten off the last st on the knitting needle, take yarn end through it, pull yarn tight and weave end back into edge of work, before cutting it off neatly.***

With cloche rib seam at centre back, position beaded triangle in centre of left side of cloche rib and stitch it into last row of rib.

Mittens

To make

Using 2¾mm (US size 2) needles, cast on 81 sts and work single (K1, P1) rib for 16cm (6in).

Next row Cast off first 26 sts, work in rib to last 26 sts, cast off rem sts. 29 sts rem on needle.

Cut off yarn and set sts aside until beads have been threaded on to yarn.

To thread beads for mitten triangle

Thread beads on to ball of yarn as for cloche triangle from ** to **.

To make beaded triangle for mitten

Using the yarn beyond the threaded beads, pick up 29 sts of mitten rib and using these sts, work beaded triangle for mitten as for beaded cloche triangle from *** to ***.

To finish

With right sides together, sew along first and last rib stitches to complete wrist rib. Starting at seam, sew a line of bead picots, as above for cloche, around cast-on edge of rib.

Starting again at seam of beaded triangle hand end, sew a similar line of picots, with a picot positioned on each side of triangle point. Attach a new thread to the point and thread on a

To finish

Using a strong thread and starting at one side of triangle, sew a continuous line of bead picots around V of triangle, using small petrol-blue beads. Make a fastening-off stitch and weave in thread ends invisibly.

To work the tassel

Work the tassel following the beading instructions on page 43.

Thread the 2 ends of thread at top of tassel into a needle and stitch into yarn at bottom point of triangle. Make one or 2 fastening-off stitches and pass needle down through top beads at top of tassel and cut off neatly. This completes the beaded cloche.

small petrol-blue bead, a large purple faceted bead, another small petrol-blue bead and 39 garnet rocailles, which will form loop to slip over middle finger of your hand.

Check that 39 rocailles is neither too large nor too small and adjust number if necessary, always keeping an odd number of beads in loop, as this creates correct shape and protects the thread from wear (fig 3).

Bring needle back through last small petrol-blue bead to starting point. Fasten off neatly and ensure that ends are woven in invisibly.

Make second mitten in same way.

fig 3

beaded denim shirt

This shirt represents a skilful combination of couched beading and appliqué. You could use it to add a unique accent to any plain fabric. It enables you to bring together fabrics, textures and colours in a way which would otherwise be difficult to achieve. Experiment further by beading a richly embellished satin appliqué motif, leaving more of the satin ground exposed, and applying this to a velvet evening jacket or throw.

You will need

Blue denim shirt
Fabric strong enough to support beaded motif (either with suitable printed motif, or to take transferred design)
Iron-on interfacing, if required
Needle fine enough to pass through beads twice when threaded
Sewing needle
Reel matching polyester thread
Reel matching sewing thread
Strong sewing thread
Tracing paper, dressmaker's carbon
Embroidery hoop or frame, large enough to contain complete motif
Rocailles (approximate quantities):
 760 dark green; 470 amber; 375 crimson; 325 scarlet; 275 gold; 245 dark amethyst; 185 leaf-green; 180 apple-green lined transparent; 170 brown; 140 pale pink rainbow; 130 crystal;100 cerise lined transparent
Round beads:
 2 6mm-diam pale green
 1 6mm-diam amber
Pearls:
 2 4mm-diam
 2 2mm-diam
 1 5mm-diam
 1 3mm-diam
Faceted crystals:
 16 2mm-diam pale green
 3 5mm-diam pale green
 3 3mm-diam amber
 2 6mm-diam pale green
 2 6mm-diam champagne
 2 6mm-diam amber
 1 5mm-diam amber
 1 3mm-diam pale green

To make up

1 Cut a piece of your chosen fabric 45 x 35cm (18 x 14in), or larger if necessary to mount it in the embroidery hoop or frame. If fabric is light to medium weight, back with iron-on interfacing.
2 Trace fruit-bowl pattern on page 108 and, using dressmaker's carbon, transfer it to centre of reverse side of fabric.
3 Stitch around edge of pattern shape using zigzag stitch, to prevent fraying when it is cut out after beading and to give a firm edge with which to appliqué beaded motif to shirt.
4 Mount prepared fabric right side up in embroidery hoop or frame, keeping warp and weft of fabric at right angles and fabric firmly stretched.
5 Thread 1 needle with 50cm (20in) approx polyester thread (for beads) and 1 with sewing thread. Referring to photograph on page 96, and using couching method detailed on page 80, begin by couching dark green stems of main leaves, and then leaves themselves. Complete fruits by beginning at outside edge and working couching inwards. Thread on appropriate number, type and colour of beads a short length at a time, and remember to pull both threads tightly while working.
6 For bunch of grapes, stitch down large beads and crystals singly first, then couch beads around them to fill in gaps between grapes. Then thread 6 or 7 small beads and stitch down to form arcs around large beads on top of couched background.
7 When beading is complete, cut carefully around zigzag stitching of pattern shape. Position beaded shape on to centre of back of blue denim shirt and pin down carefully. Appliqué to shirt fabric by stitching with very small stitches through zigzag stitching, using strong sewing thread.

Patterns & designs

This chapter shows how to chart a design for beading, as well as giving lots of additional designs for many of the techniques and projects shown earlier in the book. There are alternative designs for bookmarks and cushion trims, for bracelets and perfume bottles, for buttons and tassels. Patterns for fringing are also included, and there are decorative designs for pin-beaded baubles and wire-beaded creatures.

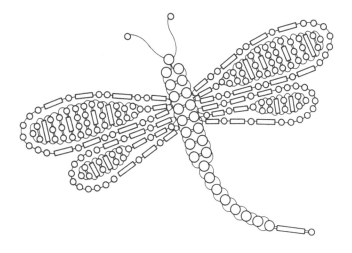

charting a design

When designing for beadwork, careful planning and drafting of a design is usually essential to ensure a perfect finished object. If you have ever missed a bead from a completed pattern you will appreciate how important accuracy is for the finished result.

You will need

A selection of squared graph paper to enable you to chart beads actual size
Tracing paper
Drafting ruler - a wide transparent ruler with a squared grid marked on to it
Graduated transparent circle template
Pair of compasses
Small set square
Very fine 0.1 or 0.2 drafting pen
Well-sharpened pencil and eraser
Selection of fine point felt tip pens and coloured pencils to colour-code beads

Charting designs

The beading technique determines the position of the beads in relation to each other. With needlewoven beading (fig 1, A), the beads hang between each other in alternate rows; with fringed beading (fig 1, B), the beads are positioned on top of each other.

By practising charting some basic design shapes for both these methods, you can see how they affect the shape. Use squared graph paper and a circle template with a fine pencil to chart some basic shapes (fig 2), using beads in between and on top of each other.

It is helpful to identify those designs which work well in a small scale, and those more effective in a larger scale before attempting to work them.

For example, in the leaf shape shown in fig 3, the smaller scale gives a crisper profile with beads worked on top of

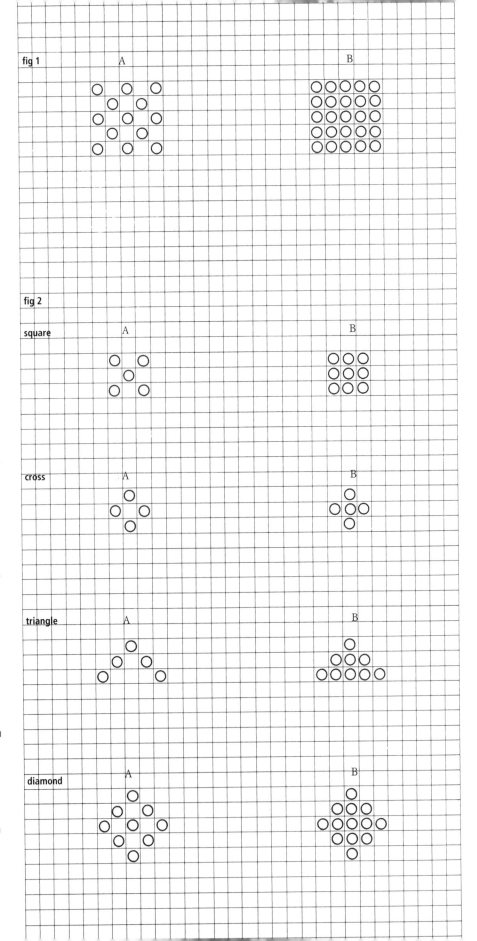

each other, rather than in between which results in a more blurred outline. A larger scale, however, gives a more effective result with beads threaded in between each other. In general, because of the diagonal line possibilities of the in between beading, the technique lends itself to geometric, rather than linear or rounded designs, which are translated more effectively by beads being on top of each other. As with all techniques, there are always the 'exceptions that break the rule', so experiment and use your own judgement. Practise drafting a variety of design shapes, either by drawing them on to the graph paper freehand, or by tracing designs and transferring them.

Colour coding charted designs

Using the beads you have selected, match the colours as closely as possible to fine felt tip pens or artists pencils. Where beads are difficult to match, choose an approximate colour. If the charted design is small enough, it is helpful to do several extra drawings to experiment with varying the bead positions and the colour balance. If the design is quite large or complicated, it might be best to make a photocopy of it to experiment.

Combining beads and bugles

Depending on the length of the bugles you are using, simply allow 2,3 or 4 graph squares to represent them, as, for example, in the simple fringe pattern shown in fig 4.

Drafting repeats

By using a transparent drafting ruler, or by dividing the graph paper into blocks, you will be able to repeat the beaded design accurately. This is helpful for fringing patterns. When you have decided on the design, make a key on the graph paper close to the charted design to indicate the bead shapes represented and a description of the different bead colours.

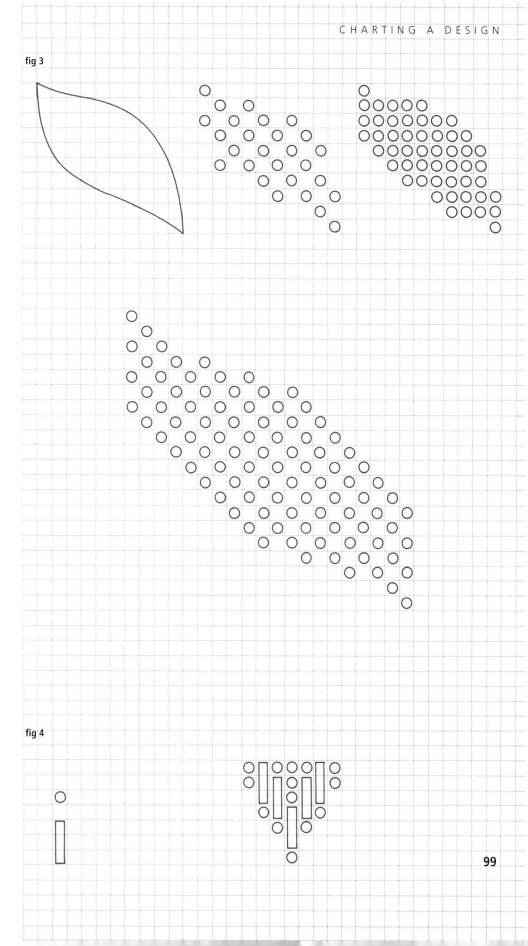

fig 3

fig 4

99

beaded bookmarks

Here are three variations on the theme of the needlewoven bookmark featured on page 15. The shaded beads are suggestions for varying colourways to emphasize the diagonal shapes that are naturally created by this technique. You can experiment by matching the beads to a variety of sumptuous ribbons, using watered silk, moiré, brocade or satin. Accentuate the quality and finish of the chosen ribbon by using a combination of matt, chalk, metallic finish or crystal beads. The final *coup de grâce* could be an extravagant drop bead. This simple beaded triangle is essentially a decorative trim and could also be used repeated on a blind or even a footstool edging.

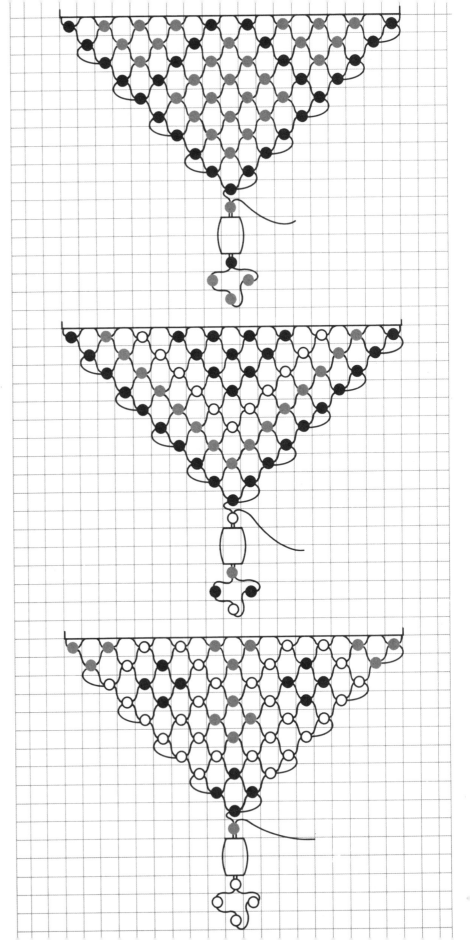

beaded trims

These are design alternatives to the edgings seen in the trimmed cushions on pages 16-21. Figs 1 and 2 involve one simple threading sequence. Figs 3 and 4 are slightly more complex, using two threading sequences. Fig 5 is the most intricate of all, with three bead threading sequences. These patterns would look lovely embellishing many soft furnishings, including decorative pillows, bolsters, curtains or valances.

fig 1

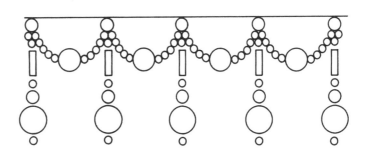

fig 2

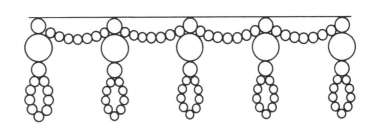

fig 3

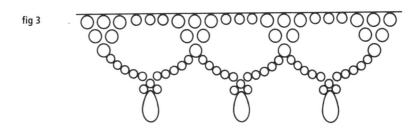

fig 4

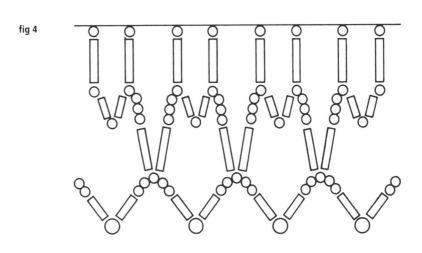

fig 5

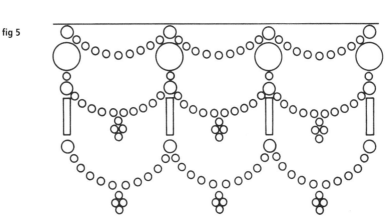

bracelets

Beaded needlewoven strips, using rocaille or faceted beads, can be used to create bracelets, chokers, and belts with a traditional feel. In Victorian times black would often have been used, with highlights in gold, silver or bronze beads. The 11-bead wide bands illustrated here give scope for many design possibilities as there is a 'middle' bead (the 6th bead) which can facilitate various colour and design possibilities. The completed beading can be further extended by an added picot of beads on each side (fig 2). The beaded fastenings can use special drops to add an extra touch of richness.

102

circular
designs

These designs involve needlewoven beading, working in rounds rather than rows. The key to success is careful manipulation of the number of beads and the tension of the working thread. We have already seen this technique used to decorative effect in the perfume bottles on pages 32-37, but most three-dimensional forms can be embellished with this age-old beading tradition – from a candlestick holder to a parchment light shade. The designs can be finished with a variety of lovely bead drops. For ease of working, the 2nd and 4th beaded rounds are shaded here.

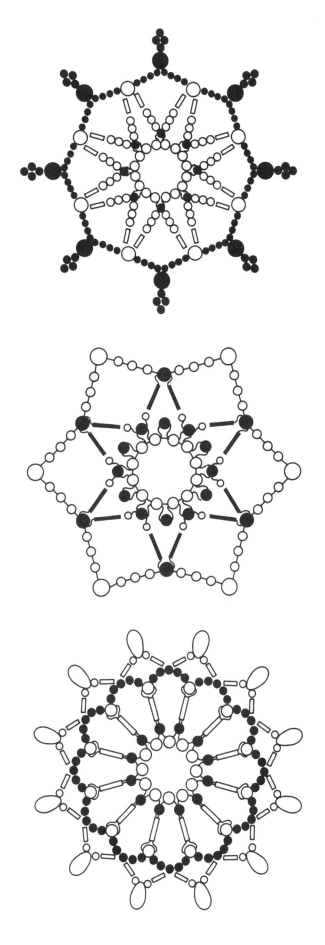

103

tassels &
buttons

One of the most popular beaded finishes of all, beaded tassels can be used to complement numerous soft furnishings, as well as items of clothing and *objets d'art*. The technique for making a basic tassel is described on page 43. The range seen here would be particularly effective worked in silk and rayon threads, creating a shining resonance and lending lustre to the finished work. Sequined buttons also make a lovely finish for soft furnishings. The final stylish touch could be a beautiful loc rosen bead at the button's centre.

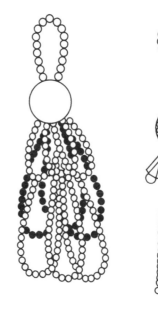
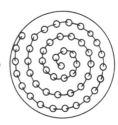

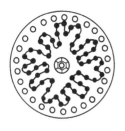
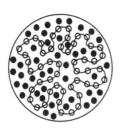

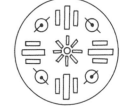

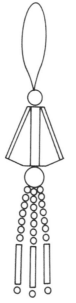

fringing patterns

The nature of bead fringing – in particular, the close proximity of the bead strings – lends itself to intense, dramatic effects. Using the technique described on pages 56-57, you can experiment with colour and shape. The shaded areas in figs 1 and 2 denote suggested coloured bead areas: fig 3 has a pansy motif integrated as part of the design. You can vary the finished shape of the fringe, ranging from a chevron finish (fig 1) to a wavy line (fig 2). Although the normal application of a fringe is usually over or in front of a light source, it can also be used to trim small bags or purses (see page 57).

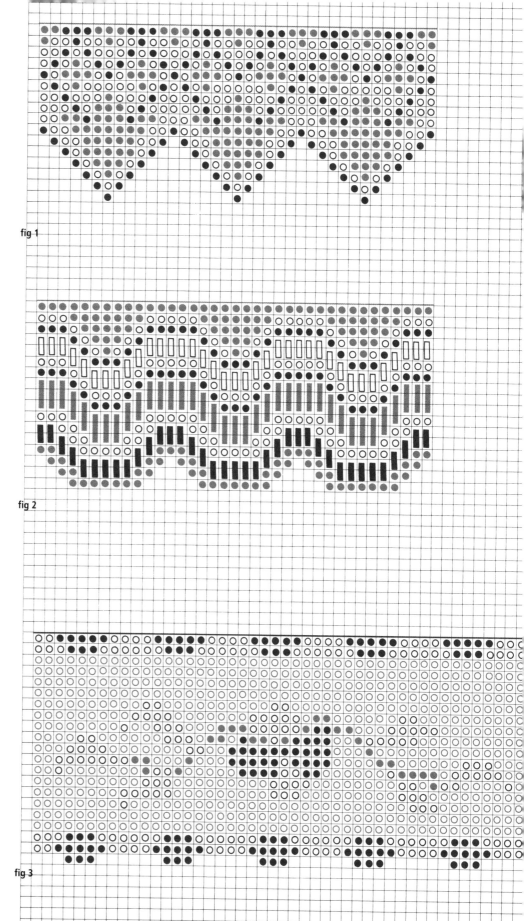

fig 1

fig 2

fig 3

- purple rocaille
- dark green rocaille
- 2mm white cut bugle
- background colour

pin-beaded baubles

Decorative, fun and festive, this collection of patterned baubles complements the designs seen on pages 68-71. For real sparkle, sequins and beads picked out in metallic shades and iridescent hues would be most effective. Simple figurative shapes or repeating geometric patterns work best.

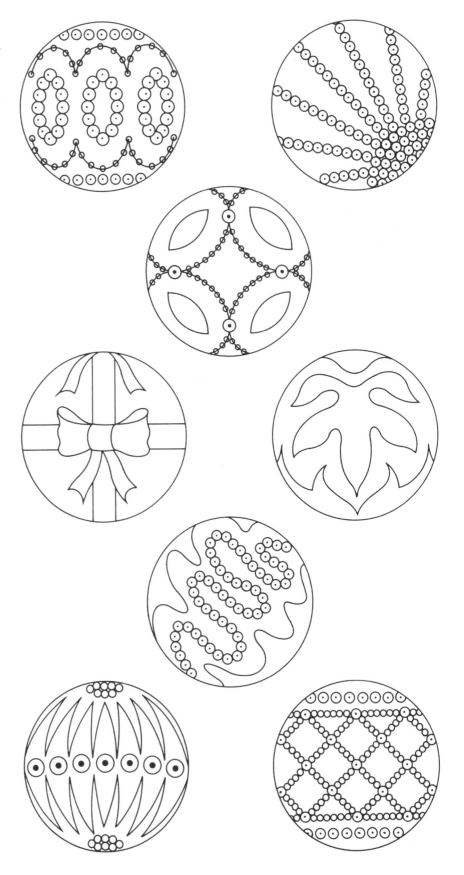

wire-beaded creatures

We have already seen wire-beading used to create beautiful beaded flowers and butterflies (see pages 72-75). Here are two delightful design alternatives. The dragonfly is made in two parts: body and wings. The enlarged detail shows how they are joined. The swift's head and body are made in one piece, worked from the beak downwards. The enlarged detail illustrates how the tail feathers are attached. Its wings are joined following the instructions for the butterfly on page 74.

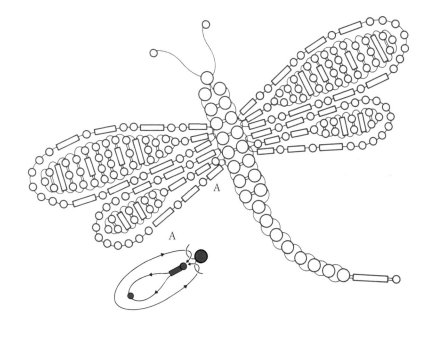

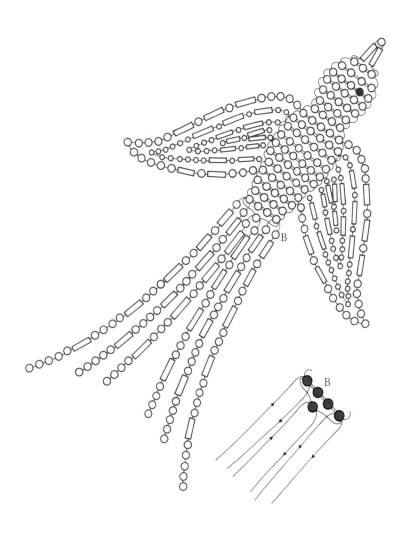

couched fruit bowl

This scaled-down appliqué motif of a fruit bowl, spilling over with fruit embellished with couched beading, is positioned beneath the bottom of the yoke on the back of the denim shirt on page 94. It works very well on denim, but any firm-woven fabric would be appropriate.

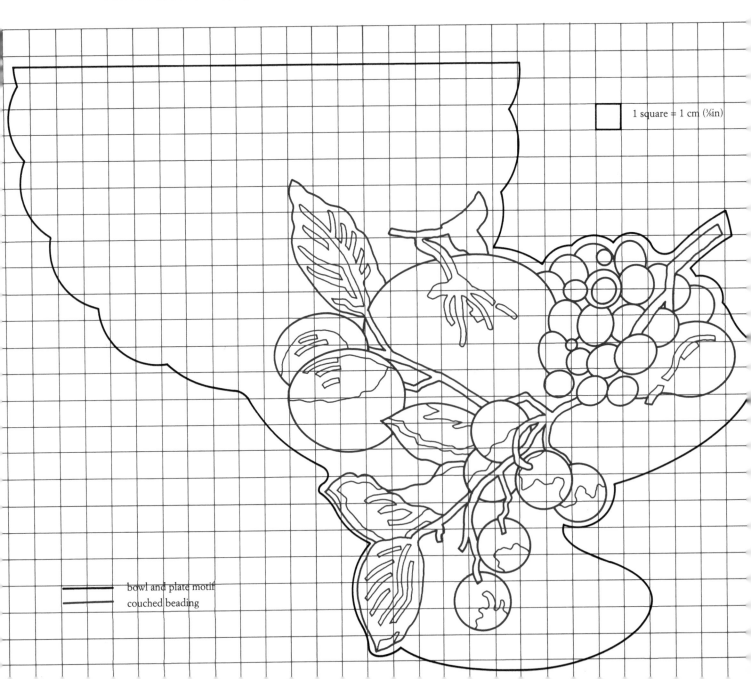

1 square = 1 cm (⅜in)

―――――― bowl and plate motif
―― ―― couched beading

beaded fruits

The instructions for these embellished fruits, complete with pips represented by sequins, are on pages 85-87. The patterns here are actual size. If you wish to alter the size, you could trace off the patterns on to graph paper and scale them up or down or use a photocopying machine to enlarge or reduce them. The pear has 3 speckle mark guides (numbered 1-3).

Other beaded fruit ideas might be a cherry, made from deep red satin and flat red sequins, or a blackberry made from satin or organza with purple, deep blue and silver flat sequins.

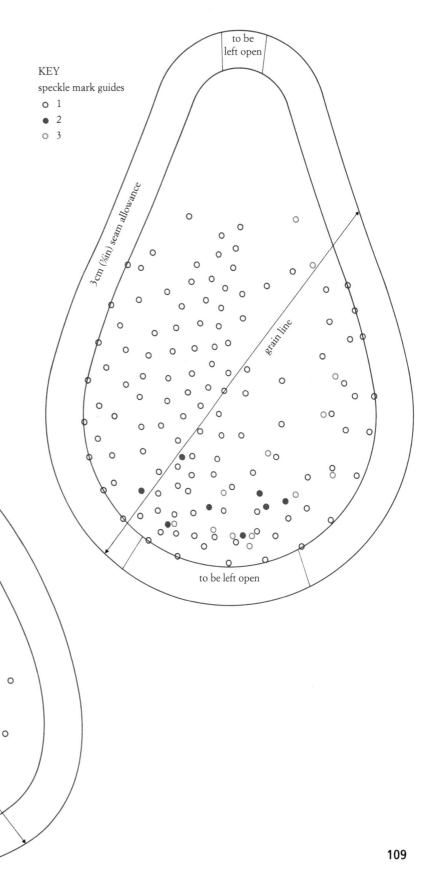

KEY
speckle mark guides
○ 1
● 2
○ 3

to be left open

3cm (⅜in) seam allowance

grain line

to be left open

3cm (⅜in) seam allowance

grain line

to be left open

index

acknowledgements

The author would like to thank the following: Alice Buck of Liberty Sewing School, Jenny Fitzgerald Bond of JLT Designs and Mercedes Sosinowicz for their friendship, advice and support.

Also for designing and making beautiful projects for the book and for their personal interest and encouragement, Candace Bahouth (Blue Poppy Cushion), Karen Spurgin (Lampshade Cover and Beaded Fruits) and Basia Zarzycka (Beaded Bolsters, Embellished Tassels and Wire-beaded Flowers).

Thanks are also due to Mary Evans, Jane O'Shea, Carey Smith, Alison Shackleton, Tim Pearce, Vanessa Courtier and all the rest of the excellent team at Quadrille who brought it all together and made it a happy experience, and to Linda Burgess for her exquisite photography.

I would also like to thank my mother and father, and Elaine and Haydon Luke, and especially Shaun Mullin, who has supported, encouraged and enabled me to develop my work over the past 25 years.

Last, but not least, J. C. Truelove for his endless support and patience, from this book's beginning to completion, and for still being there.

For the kind loan of beads for photography, the author and publisher would like to thank Ruth McCann and all at Ells & Farrier, and Karina Sterry at Hobby Horse.

Thanks are also due to pattern checker Marilyn Wilson.